Society of the Spectacle and other films

Guy Debord

Rebel Press
LONDON 1992

These filmscripts were first published by
Editions Champ Libre, Paris 1978, as part of
Oeuvres Cinématographiques Compètes: 1952-1978
by Guy Debord.

These translations published in 1992 by Rebel Press
84b Whitechapel High Street, London E1

ISBN: 0 946061 06 8

The commentary for *On the passage of a few persons through a
rather brief period of time* and *Critique of separation* are based on
those in Ken Knabb's *Situationist International anthology*,
published by Bureau of Public Secrets, 1981. No copyright.

The commentary for *Society of the Spectacle* is based on the
revised translation of the book of the same name, first
published by Black and Red, Detroit, 1977. No copyright.

*Refutation of all judgements whether for or against, which have
been brought to date on the film 'Society of the Spectacle'* is based
on the translation by Ken Sanborn, New York, 1989. No
copyright for non-profit editions.

Other translations, and amendments to the above, by Richard
Parry. No copyright.

Rebel Press would like to thank Malcolm Hopkins and
Clifford Harper for their help and advice in producing this
edition.

Printed by
Aldgate Press, London

Contents

Introduction

When Guy Debord's publisher, Gerard Lebovici, was assassi-
nated in mysterious circumstances on 5 March 1984, Debord
resolved never to allow his films to be shown again in France.
For Debord, this murder was no coincidence, but a matter
directly attributable to the clandestine forces in existence within
the French state — forces similar to neo-fascist groups in Italy
or death-squads in El Salvador.

This was not mere paranoia on Debord's part. Lebovici's murder happened within weeks of the publication by Champ Libre
of the autobiography of Jacques Mesrine, France's most notori-
ous criminal since the anarchist bank-robber Jules Bonnot. Mesrine had run rings around the police for years, and was becoming increasingly interested in radical politics: for the state, such
a conjuncture had to be avoided and such an embarrassment
eliminated.

Mesrine was machine-gunned to death by a special police execution squad in a Parisian back-street on 2 November 1979. It
was understood that the police would not take kindly to anyone
daring to publish his autobiography, but Lebovici took the risk.
It was to prove fatal. Incensed at his murder and the deliberate
lack of any serious investigation into it, Debord expressed his
outrage by refusing to let any of his films be shown again in
France.

Their existence has therefore remained somewhat obscure, although the full scripts were published in French in 1978. No full
translations have been published in English previously, and we

present here the full texts of the first five of Debord's films. His sixth and last film, whose title is taken from the celebrated mediaeval palindrome (*In girum imus nocte et consumimur igni — We spin round in the night and are consumed by fire*), is already separately available in English.

Debord's first venture into film, at the age of 21, was part of his involvement with the Lettrist Movement, a group of *avant-garde* artists whose leading light was Isidore Isou. In 1950, the year that Debord joined, Isou's film *The drivel and eternity treatise* was awarded best *avant-garde* film prize at Cannes by Jean Cocteau. Two years later Debord produced an even more radical gesture against the concept of cinema in *Howlings in favour of Sade*, a film that not only had an occasional soundtrack of seemingly random and unrelated dialogue (much like Isou's film), but which was without any images, and boasted substantial periods where the screen remained completely dark and there was no sound whatsoever. This film was dedicated to Gil J. Wolman, another Lettrist, a couple of years older than Debord, who had also produced his own film, *The Anti-concept*.

After splitting with Isou in 1952, it was Debord, his partner Michelle Bernstein, and Wolman who formed the core of the Lettrist International, within whose ranks were developed the concepts of unitary urbanism, the creation of situations, detournement, psychogeography and the derive. These concerns were reflected in Debord's next two films, *On the passage of a few persons through a rather brief period of time* (1959) and *Critique of separation* (1961). They were shot in the early years of the Situationist International, which had been founded in 1957 through a merger of the mainly Paris-based Lettrist International with Scandinavian, German and English *avant-garde* groups. The first film is a commentary on the experiences of the *Lettristes* and opens with shots of their favourite stomping grounds: the Left Bank, les Halles and the Ile Saint Louis. It is a very personal film concerned with their subjective experience of alienation and their first gropings towards a liberation of everyday life.

Certain of the contemporary "decomposition and exhaustion of individual expression", Debord used a plagiarism of images to form an "accumulation of detourned elements" taken from advertisements, newsclips and cinema: the perfect complement, in terms of images, to his dual exploration of the alienation of people in relation to each other and themselves, as much as from their environment. Debord and Wolman had already decided, writing in 1956, that it was "obviously in the realm of cinema that detournement can attain its greatest efficacity".

Both films were 20 minutes long, shot in 35mm black and white in Paris in a few weeks, and edited a few months later.

Debord did not make another film until 1973, a year after the demise of the SI and twelve since his last excursion into cinema. Following the 1962 split between the artistically-inclined Scandinavian situationists and the increasingly 'politically-concerned' members centred around Debord and the French section, the SI lived through its 'heroic years': 1965 — publication of *The Revolution of Everyday Life*; 1966 — the Strasbourg scandal; 1967 — publication of *Society of the Spectacle*; culminating in the events of May '68, apogee of the SI's influence.

In his film *Society of the Spectacle* Debord was attempting to make a theoretical film, a dialectical complement to his earlier explorations into the realm of subjective alienation. However, he continued to use the same 'cut-up' technique through a detournement of newsclips, adverts and fragments of famous films

8

such as *Battleship Potemkin*, *Johnny Guitar* and *For Whom the Bell Tolls*, to name but a few. The same sort of montage was also employed for his last two films shot in 1975 and 1978. *Society of the Spectacle* was perhaps his most demanding film to date, being feature length, and containing a commentary of just over one third of the text from the original book, interspersed with quotations from Marx, Machiavelli, Clausewitz and others.

Debord's highly innovative attempt at a theoretical film threw down a challenge that has not been taken up, despite the twenty years that have elapsed; only one small group from America, using video, having tried a similar theoretical critique of the modern world in *Call it Sleep*. Indeed, looking at the whole of Debord's cinematographic *oeuvre*, what is still striking after all these years is the radicality of the content and the innovation of the technique for each of the three periods: 1952 (Lettrist); 1959-61 (early Situationist); and 1973-5 (post-Situationist). I hope that something of this freshness and vitality comes through in the translations you are about to read.

Richard Parry

Howlings
in favour of Sade

1952
FILMS LETTRISTES

Voice 1   The film by Guy-Ernest Debord, *Howlings in fa-vour of Sade...*

Voice 2:   *Howlings in favour of Sade* is dedicated to Gil J Wolman.

Voice 3:   Article 115. When a person shall have ceased to appear at his place of abode or home address for four years, and about whom there has been no news whatsoever, the interested parties shall be able to petition the lower court in order that his or her absence be declared.

Voice 1:   Love is only worthwhile in a pre-revolutionary period.

Voice 2:   None of them love you, you liar! Art begins, grows and disappears because frustrated men bypass the world of official expression and the festivals of its poverty.

Voice 4:   Say, did you sleep with Françoise?
(young girl)

Voice 1:   What a time! Memorandum for a history of cine-ma: 1902—*Journey to the Moon.* 1920—*The Cabinet of Doctor Caligari.* 1924—*Entr'acte.* 1926—*Battle-ship Potemkin.* 1928—*Un Chien Andalou.* 1931—

12

City Lights. Birth of Guy-Ernest Debord. 1951—
The drivel and eternity treatise. 1952—*The Anti-concept.*—*Howlings in favour of Sade.*

Voice 5:   "Just as the film was about to start, Guy-Ernest
Debord would climb on stage to say a few words
by way of introduction. He'd say simply: 'There's
no film. Cinema is dead. There can't be film any
more. If you want, let's have a discussion'."

Voice 3:   Article 516. All property is either movable or
immovable.

Voice 2:   In order never to be alone again.

Voice 1:   She is ugliness and beauty. She is like everything
that we love today.

Voice 2:   The art of the future will be the overturning of
situations or nothing.

Voice 3:   In the cafés of Saint-Germain-des-Prés!

Voice 1:   You know, I like you very much.

Voice 3:   An important Lettrist commando made up of
some thirty members, all donning the filthy uniform that is their only really original trademark,

turned up at the Croisette with the firm desire of indulging in some scandal capable of drawing attention to themselves.

Voice 1:   Happiness is a new idea in Europe.

Voice 5:   "I only know about the actions of men, but in my eyes men are transposed, one for the other. In the final analysis, works alone differentiate us."

Voice 1:   And their revolts became conformisms.

Voice 3:   Article 488. The age of majority is fixed at twenty-one years; at that age one is capable of all acts of civil life.

SILENCE FOR TWO MINUTES DURING WHICH THE SCREEN REMAINS DARK.

Voice 4:
(young girl)   His memory always rediscovered it, in a flash, as if burnished by fireworks on contact with water.

Voice 1:   He knew quite well that nothing of his exploits remained in a town that rotated with the Earth, as the Earth rotated in the Galaxy, which is itself only a tiny part of a little island which recedes away from us to infinity.

Voice 2: All black, eyes closed to the excess of disaster.

SILENCE FOR ONE MINUTE DURING WHICH THE SCREEN REMAINS DARK.

Voice 1: A science of situations is to be created, which will borrow elements from psychology, statistics, urbanism and ethics. These elements have to run together to an absolutely new conclusion: the conscious creation of situations.

SILENCE FOR THIRTY SECONDS DURING WHICH THE SCREEN REMAINS DARK.

Voice 1: A few lines from a newspaper from 1950: "A leading young radio actress threw herself into the River Isère, Grenoble. Young Madeleine Reineri aged twelve and a half, who, under the pseudonym of Pirouette, used to liven up the radio program 'Happy Thursdays' on the Alpes-Grenoble station, threw herself into the Isère on Friday afternoon having placed her satchel on the river bank."

Voice 2: My little sister, we are nothing to look at. The Isère and *la misère* continue. We are powerless.

SILENCE FOR ONE MINUTE, THIRTY SECONDS, DUR-
ING WHICH THE SCREEN REMAINS DARK.

Voice 4:   But no-one's talking about Sade in this film.
(young girl)

Voice 1:   The cold of interstellar space, thousands of de-
grees below freezing point or absolute zero Fahr-
enheit or Centigrade; the first indicators of dawn
approaching. The hurried passage of Jacques
Vaché through the clouds of war, that extraordinary driving force inside him, that catastrophic
haste which destroyed him; the rude lashing of
Arthur Cravan, himself swallowed up at that time
in the Bay of Mexico...

Voice 3:   Article 1793. When an architect or a businessman
is given a contract for the construction of a build-
ing according to a plan agreed to by the landowner, he cannot demand a higher price either on
account of an increase in the workforce or materi-
als, or due to any changes or additions made to
the plan, unless such changes, additions or increases have been authorised in writing, and the
price agreed with the landowner.

Voice 2:   The perfection of suicide is in ambiguity.

16

SILENCE FOR FIVE MINUTES DURING WHICH THE SCREEN REMAINS DARK.

Voice 2:   What is a love that's unique?

Voice 3:   I will only answer in the presence of my lawyer.

SILENCE FOR ONE MINUTE DURING WHICH THE SCREEN REMAINS DARK.

Voice 1:   Order reigns, it doesn't govern.

SILENCE FOR TWO MINUTES DURING WHICH THE SCREEN REMAINS DARK.

Voice 2:   The first marvel is to come before her without knowing how to talk to her. The hands of the female prisoners move no faster than race horses filmed in slow-motion, as they touch her mouth and her breast. In all innocence the ropes become water and we flow together towards the day.

Voice 4:   I believe we'll never see each other again.
(young girl)

Voice 2:   Near a kiss, the lights of the winter street will end.

Voice 4:
(young girl)

Paris was very nice thanks to the transport strike.

Voice 2:

Jack the Ripper was never caught.

Voice 4:
(young girl)

It's funny, the telephone.

Voice 2:

What defiant love, as Madame de Ségur used to say.

Voice 4:
(young girl)

I will tell you some stories from my country which are very frightening, but they have to be told at night in order to be frightening.

Voice 2:

My dear Ivich, the Chinese neighbourhoods are unfortunately less populous than you think. You are 15 years old. One day the most fashionable colours will no longer be worn.

Voice 4:
(young girl)

I knew you already.

Voice 2:

The drift of the continents pushes you further apart every day. The virgin forest has moved less than you.

Voice 4:
(young girl)
Guy, another minute and it'll be tomorrow.

Voice 2:
The Demon of Arms. You remember. That's it. No-
body satisfies us. All the same... The hail on the
banners of glass. We will remember it, that planet.

SILENCE FOR FOUR MINUTES DURING WHICH THE
SCREEN REMAINS DARK.

Voice 2:
You will see that they will be famous later! I will
never accept the scandalous and scarcely credible
fact of the existence of a police force. Several
cathedrals have been erected to the memory of
Serge Berna. Love is only worthwhile in a pre-revolutionary period. I made this film while there
was still enough time left to talk about it. Jean-Isi-
dore, in order to get out of that transient crowd.
On Gabriel-Pomerand Square when we've grown
old. The little skivers all had glorious futures in
the school and college systems.

SILENCE FOR THREE MINUTES DURING WHICH THE
SCREEN REMAINS DARK.

Voice 2:
There are still many people that morality makes
neither laugh nor cry.

Voice 3:   Article 489. The adult who is in a constant state of imbecility, dementia, or mad rage must be detained even though his state allows for intervals of lucidity.

Voice 2:   So close, so gently, I lose myself in the meaninglessness of language. I push into you, you're wide open, it's easy. It's like a hot stream. It's as smooth as a sea of oil. It's like a forest fire.

Voice 1:   It's cinema!

Voice 3:   The Parisian police force is thirty thousand truncheons strong.

SILENCE FOR FOUR MINUTES DURING WHICH THE SCREEN REMAINS DARK.

Voice 2:   "The poetic worlds close up and forget by themselves." In a corner of the night the sailors are making war, and the ships in bottles are for you who loved them. You lay yourself down on the beach as hands more loving than the rain, the wind and the thunder play under your dress every evening. Life is great in Cannes in the summer. Rape, which is forbidden, becomes banale in our memories. "When we were on the Shenandoah." Yes. Of course.

20

Voice 1: And these resigned faces, which once bore flashes of desire like ink splattered on a wall, were like shooting stars. Let gin, rum and brandy flow like the Great Armada. This for the funeral oration. But all those people were so commonplace.

SILENCE FOR FIVE MINUTES DURING WHICH THE SCREEN REMAINS DARK.

Voice 1: We've had a narrow escape.

Voice 2: The most beautiful is still to come, otherwise death would taste like a raw steak. And wet hair on the beach which is too hot and which is our silence.

Voice 1: But he's a Jew!

Voice 2: We were ready to blow up all the bridges, but the bridges let us down.

SILENCE FOR FOUR MINUTES DURING WHICH THE SCREEN REMAINS DARK.

Voice 1: Young Madeleine Reineri, aged twelve and a half, who under the pseudonym of Pirouette used to liven up the radio programme 'Happy Thurs-

days' on the Alpes-Grenoble station, threw herself into the Isère.

Voice 2:   Mademoiselle Reineri, in that quarter of Europe,
             you will always have your surprised face and that
             body, the best of promised lands. Like neon light,
             words repeat their banal truths.

Voice 1:   I love you.

Voice 4:   It must be terrible to die.
(young girl)

Voice 1:   See you.

Voice 4:   You drink far too much.
(young girl)

Voice 1:   What are childish love affairs?

Voice 4:   I don't know what you're talking about.
(young girl)

Voice 1:   I knew it. And there was a time when I regretted
             it very much.

Voice 4:   Do you want an orange?
(young girl)

Voice 1:   The beautiful tearing apart of the volcanic islands.

Voice 4:   In the past.
(young girl)

Voice 1:   I've nothing more to say to you.

Voice 2:   After all the answers at the wrong time, and youth getting older, night falls again from on high.

SILENCE FOR THREE MINUTES DURING WHICH THE SCREEN REMAINS DARK.

Voice 2:   We live like lost children, our adventures incomplete.

SILENCE FOR TWENTY-FOUR MINUTES DURING WHICH THE SCREEN REMAINS DARK.

On the passage of
a few persons
through a rather brief
period of time

1959
DANSK-FRANSK
EXPERIMENTALFILMSKOMPAGNI

Voice 1:
(male
announcer)

This neighbourhood was made for the wretched

Facades of buildings in the neighbourhood of Saint-Germain-des-

Sub-title: Paris 1952

dignity of the *petit-bourgeoisie,* for respectable oc-

Prés.

cupations and intellectual tourism. The sedentary
population of the upper floors was sheltered from
the influences of the street. This neighbourhood

Young people pass by.

has remained the same. It was the strange setting
for our story. Here, a systematic questioning of all

A photograph of two couples drinking wine at a

Handel: Formal love theme.

the diversions and works of a society, a total

table in a café is studied by the camera in the style of an art-film.

critique of its idea of happiness, was expressed in
acts.

These people also scorned 'subjective profund-
ity'. They were interested in nothing but an adequate and concrete expression of themselves.

Voice 2:
(Debord,
monotone)

Human beings are not fully conscious of their real
life...usually groping in the dark; overwhelmed
by the consequences of their acts; at every moment groups and individuals find themselves
confronted with results they have not wished.

The music is interrupted.

Voice 1: They said that oblivion was their ruling passion.
Other faces.

They wanted to reinvent everything each day; to become masters and possessors of their own lives.

Just as one does not judge a man according to the conception he has of himself, one cannot judge such periods of transition according to their own consciousness; on the contrary, one must explain the consciousness through the material conditions of material life, through the conflict between social conditions and the forces of social produc-
The Pope and other ecclesiastics.
tion.

The progress achieved in the domination of nature was not yet matched by the corresponding liberation of everyday life. Youth passed away
Young girls coming out of school.
among the various controls of resignation.
French police in the street.

Our camera has captured for you a few aspects of
A sequence in reportage style of café tables in Saint-Germain-
a provisional micro-society.
des-Prés.

The knowledge of empirical facts remains ab-

stract and superficial as long as it is not concret-
ized by its integration into the whole — which
alone permits the supersession of partial and abstract problems so as to arrive at their CONCRETE
ESSENCE, and implicitly at their meaning.

This group was on the margins of the economy. It
tended toward a role of pure consumption, and
first of all the free consumption of its time. It thus
found itself directly engaged in qualitative variations of daily life but deprived of any means to
intervene in them.

The group ranged over a very small area. The
Night-time in Les Halles.
same times brought them back to the same places.
No one went to bed early. Discussion on the
Panoramic view over a very lively and packed square in Les Halles
meaning of all this continued...
at night.

Voice 2:   "Our life is a journey — In the winter and the
              night. — We seek our passage..."

Voice 1:   The abandoned literature nevertheless exerted a
              Several views of dawn over Les Halles.
              delaying action on new affective formulations.

28

Voice 2:   There was the fatigue and the cold of the morning in this much-traversed labyrinth, like an enigma that we had to resolve. It was a looking-glass reality through which we had to discover the possible richness of reality. On the bank of the

Paris — The River Seine look-

Delalande: Noble and tragic

river, evening began once again; and caresses;

ing east.   *Piles of bricks on the*

theme for solo bassoon.

Quai Saint-Bernard.

and the importance of a world without import-ance. Just as the eyes have a blurred vision of many things and can see only one clearly, so the will can strive only incompletely toward diverse objects and can completely love only one at a time.

A girl.

The music dies down.

Voice 3:   No one counted on the future. It would never be
(young girl)   *Inside the labyrinth of bricks.*

possible to be together later, or anywhere else.

Police vans depart.   *The Ile Saint-Louis at dusk.*

There would never be a greater freedom.

Two very young couples dancing on a beach next to a guitar player.

Voice 1:   The refusal of time and growing old, automat-

Some locations between Place Saint Sulpice and rue Mazarine.

ically limited encounters in this narrow contin-
gent zone, where what was lacking was felt as
irreparable. The extreme precariousness of the
means of getting by without working was at the
root of this impatience, which made excesses necessary and breaks definitive.

Voice 2:   One never really contests an organization of ex-

THE SCREEN REMAINS WHITE.

istence without contesting all of that organization's forms of language.

Voice 1:   When freedom is practised in a closed circle, it

Tracking shots in a café, the camera's movement arbitrarily cut by

Delalande: Allegro of court music.

fades into a dream, becomes a mere represent-

boards: "The passions and celebrations of a violent age"; "In the

ation of itself. The ambience of play is by nature

course of movement and accordingly on the transitory side"; "The

unstable. At any moment 'ordinary life' can pre-

most exciting suspense!"

vail once again. The geographical limitation of
play is even more striking than its temporal limitation. Any game takes place within the contours

of its spatial domain. Around the neighbourhood,

Board: "With marvellous decor spe-

around its fleeting and threatened immobility,

cially made for the purpose!"

stretched a half-known city where people met

People pass along the Boulevard Saint-Michel in foggy weather.

The music fades out.

only by chance, losing their way forever. The girls

A couple at

there, because they were legally under the control

a table in a café.

of their families until the age of eighteen, were
often recaptured by the defenders of that detest-

In Japan several hundred police come into view running.

able institution. They were generally confined

The outside walls of the Che-

under the guard of those creatures who among all

villy-Larue prison.

the bad products of a bad society are the most
ugly and repugnant: nuns.

What usually makes documentaries so easy to

THE SCREEN REMAINS WHITE.

understand is the arbitrary limitation of their subject matter. They describe the atomisation of social functions and the isolation of their products.

One can, in contrast, envisage the entire complexity of a moment which is not resolved into a work, a moment whose movement indissolubly contains facts and values whose meaning does not yet appear. The subject matter of the documentary would then be this confused totality.

Voice 2:   The epoch had arrived at the level of knowledge

Violent confrontations between Japanese workers and the police.

and technical means that made possible, and in-

General view of events. The police slowly gain ground.

creasingly necessary, a DIRECT construction of all aspects of a liberated, affective and practical existence. The appearance of these superior means of action, still unused because of the delays in the project of liquidating the commodity economy, had already condemned aesthetic activity, whose ambitions and powers were both outdated. The decay of art and of all values of former mores had formed our sociological background. The ruling class's monopoly over the instruments we had to

THE SCREEN REMAINS WHITE.

control in order to realize the collective art of our time had excluded us from a cultural production officially devoted to illustrating and repeating the past. An art film on this generation can only be a film on its absence of real works.

Everyone unthinkingly followed the paths learn-

People pass by in front of the railings of the Cluny Museum.

ed once and for all, to their work and their homes, to their predictable future. For them duty had already become a habit, and a habit a duty. They did not see the deficiency of their city. They thought the deficiency of their life was natural. We wanted to break out of this conditioning, in

Windows lit up at night in the Rue des Ecoles and the Rue

Handel: Formal love theme.

quest of another use of the urban landscape, in

Montagne-Sainte-Geneviève.

quest of new passions. The atmosphere of a few places gave us intimations of the future powers of an architecture it would be necessary to create to be the support and framework for less mediocre games. We could expect nothing of anything we

The music ends.

ourselves had not altered. The urban environ-

Some houses in Paris.

ment proclaimed the orders and tastes of the ruling society just as violently as the newspapers. It is man who makes the unity of the world, but man has extended himself everywhere. Men can see nothing around them that is not their own image; everything speaks to them of themselves. Their very landscape is alive. There were obstacles everywhere. There was a coherence in the ob-

English police on foot and on horseback drive back demonstrators.

stacles of all types. They maintained the coherent
reign of poverty. Everything being connected, it

THE SCREEN REMAINS WHITE.

was necessary to CHANGE EVERYTHING by a unitary struggle, or nothing. It was necessary to link
up with the masses, but we were surrounded by
sleep.

Voice 3:
(young girl)
The dictatorship of the proletariat is a desperate
struggle, bloody and bloodless, violent and
peaceful, military and economic, educational and
administrative, against the forces and traditions
of the old world.

Voice 1:
In this country it is once again the men of order

A demonstration of white colonists in Algiers, May 1958. General

who have rebelled. They have reinforced their

Massu and General Salan. A company of parachutists marches

power. They have been able to aggravate the grot-

towards the camera.

esqueness of the ruling conditions according to
their will. They have embellished their system
with the funereal ceremonies of the past.

General De Gaulle speaks on a rostrum and bangs his fist.

Voice 2:   Years, like a single instant prolonged to this point,

THE SCREEN REMAINS WHITE.

come to an end.

Voice 1:   That which was directly lived reappears frozen in

The star of an advertising film Monsavon.   A girl's face.

the distance, fitted into the tastes and illusions of an era carried away with it.

A cavalry charge in the streets of a town.

Voice 2:   The appearance of events that we had not made,

THE SCREEN REMAINS WHITE.

that others have made against us, obliges us from now on to be aware of the passage of time, its results, the transformation of our own desires into events. What differentiates the past from the pres-

The face of another girl.

ent is precisely its out-of-reach objectivity; there is no more should-be; being is so consumed that

A starlette in a bath.

it has ceased to exist. The details are already lost in the dust of time. Who was afraid of life, afraid

Film of a solar eruption.   Tracking shot of the starlette in the

of the night, afraid of being taken, afraid of being

bath.   The solar eruption shot continues its rising movement.

kept?

Voice 3:   That which should be abolished continues, and

In Japan a dozen police with helmets and gasmasks continue to

we continue to wear away with it. We are en-

advance across a large space, now cleared, slowly firing tear-gas

gulfed. We are separated. The years pass and we

grenades.

have not changed anything.

Voice 2:   Once again morning in the same streets. Once

Day breaks over a Paris bridge.   Slow panorama across

Delalande: Noble and tragic theme (reprise).

again the fatigue of so many similarly passed

the Place des Victoires at dawn.

nights. It is a walk that has lasted a long time.

The music dies down.

Voice 1:   Really hard to drink more.

THE SCREEN REMAINS WHITE.

Voice 2:   Of course one might make a film of it. But even if

A film crew around a camera.

such a film succeeds in being as fundamentally

The tracking shot

incoherent and unsatisfying as the reality it deals

across the café, as seen before, but uncut and with a series of faults:

with, it will never be more than a re-creation —

people getting into the edge of the frame, reflections on the lens,

36

poor and false like this botched tracking shot.

camera shadow, with a panorama drawn out at the end of the shot.

Voice 3:   There are now people who flatter themselves that

THE SCREEN REMAINS WHITE.

they are authors of films, as others were authors of novels. They are even more backward than the novelists because they are ignorant of the decomposition and exhaustion of individual expression in our time, ignorant of the end of the arts of passivity. They are praised for their sincerity since they dramatize, with more personal depth, the conventions of which their life consists. There is talk of the liberation of the cinema. But what does it matter to us if one more art is liberated through which Pierre or Jacques or François can joyously express their slave sentiments? The only interesting venture is the liberation of everyday life, not only in the perspectives of history but for us and right away. This entails the withering away of alienated forms of communication. The cinema too has to be destroyed.

Voice 2:   In the final analysis, stars are created by the need

A car stops. Tracking shot of the star of Monsavon *coming*

we have for them, and not by talent or absence of

downstairs.

talent or even by the film industry or advertising.

Two images of the film's clapperboard recorded for two shots already

Miserable need, dismal, anonymous life that

seen.

would like to expand itself to the dimensions of cinema life. The imaginary life on the screen is the

Horseriders in the Bois de Boulogne.

product of this real need. The star is the projection of this need.

The images of the advertisements during the in-

The advertising starlette shows how much she likes the soap and

termissions are more suited than any others for

smiles to the audience.

evoking an intermission of life.

To really describe this era it would no doubt be

THE SCREEN REMAINS WHITE UNTIL THIRTY SECONDS AFTER THE

necessary to show many other things. But what

LAST WORD IS SPOKEN.

would be the point? Better to grasp the totality of what has been done and what remains to be done than to add more ruins to the old world of the spectacle and of memories.

Human beings are not fully conscious of their real life...usually groping in the dark; overwhelmed by the consequences of their acts.

At every moment groups and individuals find themselves confronted with results they have not wished.

The ambiance of play is by nature unstable. At any moment 'ordinary life' can prevail once again.

Around the neighbourhood, around its fleeting and threatened immobility, stretched a half-known city where people met only by chance...

"Our life is a journey — In the winter and the night. — We seek our passage..."

Stars are created by the need we have for them. Miserable need...

Critique
of separation

1961
DANSK-FRANSK
EXPERIMENTALFILMSKOMPAGNI

We don't know what to say. Words form themselves into se-

Tracking shot over a group of people on a café terrace. The camera, hand-held as if in

quences and gestures recognise each other. Outside us. Of

a news report, moves towards Debord who is talking to a very young brunette.

course some methods are mastered, some results verified. It's

General view of the two of them walking off together.

often pleasant. But so many things we have wanted have not

Another girl, blonde.

been attained; or only partially and not like we thought. What
communication have we desired, or experienced, or only simu-

Cartoon-strip: Blonde-haired girl looking

lated? What true project has been lost?

exhausted. Caption: "But it had failed, the jeep was too deeply bogged down in the liquid mud of the swamp..."

The cinematic spectacle has its rules, which enable one to pro-

360 degree panorama shot from the Saint-Merri plateau.

Sub-title: Halfway on the path of life

Couperin: March of the Champagne Regiment.

duce satisfactory products. But dissatisfaction is the reality that
must be taken as a point of departure. The function of the

I found myself again in a dark forest

cinema is to present a false, isolated coherence, dramatic or
documentary, as a substitute for a communication and an activity that are absent. To demystify documentary cinema it is

where the right way had been lost.

necessary to dissolve what is called its subject matter.

End of the March.

A well-established rule is that anything in a film that is said

Cartoon-strip: A diver thinks: "Without the lifeline and without air I won't last long.

other than by way of images must be repeated or else the

If only I could free myself from these weights..."   *High angle shot*

spectators will miss it. That may be true. But this sort of incom-

in a bar. A couple enter, shut the door, and advance.

prehesion is present everywhere in everyday encounters.
Something must be specified, made clear, but there's not
enough time and you are not sure of having been understood.
Before you have done or said what was necessary, you've

A still shot taken from a film: A US marine radio operator. Behind him stands an

Sub-title: Do you read me? Do you read me? Come in, come in...

already gone. Across the street. Overseas. There will never be

officer and the heroine.

Over and out!

another chance.

After all the dead time and lost moments, there remain these

View over Place de la Concorde from a helicopter.

endlessly traversed postcard landscapes; this distance or-

The Seine running through the centre of Paris.

ganised between each and everyone. Childhood? It's right here;
we've never left it.

Our epoch accumulates powers and dreams of itself as being

Close-up of a rocket taking off.

rational. But no one recognises these powers as his own. There

General view of the take-off.

is no entering into adulthood: only the possible transformation,
someday, of this long restlessness into a routine somnolence.
Because no one ceases to be held under guardianship. The

A pilot equipped for the stratosphere. An officer with drawn sabre.

problem is not that people live more or less poorly; but that they

Shot of the cover of a science fiction book.

live in a way that is always out of their control.

At the same time, it is a world in which we have been taught

A pinball machine; the movement of the ball.

change. Nothing stops. It changes more every day; and I know
that those who day after day produce it against themselves can
appropriate it for themselves.

The only adventure, we said, is to contest the totality, whose

A still from a film: A king and knights around the Round Table.

Bodin de Boismortier: Allegro movement, Op.37 — Concerto in E Minor in
five parts.

centre is this way of living, where we can test our strength but

Sub-title: To give every person the social space essential for the expression

not use it. In reality no adventure is directly formed for us. The

Two situationists.

of life.

adventures form part of the whole range of legends transmitted

One knight defies another in a picture from a Hollywood-style film.

by cinema or in other ways; part of the whole spectacular sham

A situationist drinking a glass of wine.

of history.

General view of a group sitting at a table in a cafe in Montagne-Sainte-Geneviève.

Sub-title: If Man is created by circumstance, one must create human circumstances.

Sub-title: Comrades, unitary urbanism is dynamic, that is to say it is in direct relationship with modes of behaviour.

Until the environment is collectively dominated, there will be

Other situationists.

Sub-title: Passions have been interpreted enough. It's a question now of

no individuals — only spectres haunting the things anarchically

finding new ones.

presented to them by others. In chance situations we meet separated people moving randomly. Their divergent emotions

The girl from the opening shot passes by.   *Panoramic aerial view of the centre*

neutralise each other and maintain their solid environment of

of Paris.

boredom. As long as we are unable to make our own history, to freely create situations, the effort toward unity will introduce other separations. The quest for a central activity leads to the formation of new specialisations.

And only a few encounters were like signals emanating from a

The quarrelling knights again.   *The same girl again.*

The music dies away.

more intense life, a life that has not really been found.

What cannot be forgotten reappears in dreams. At the end of

Alternating tracking shots: the face of the girl; an aeroplane gets further away after

this type of dream, half asleep, the events are still for a brief

taking off from the snow-covered countryside.

moment taken as real. And the reactions they give rise to become clearer, more distinct, more reasonable; like so many mornings, the memory of what one drank the night before. Then comes the awareness that it's all false, that 'it was only a dream', that there are no new realities and no going back into it. Nothing you can hold on to. These dreams are flashes from the unresolved past. They unilaterally illuminate moments previously lived in confusion and doubt. They strikingly publicise those of our needs that have not been answered. Here is daylight, and

Panoramic view over the

Boismortier: reprise of the Allegro.

here are perspectives that now no longer mean anything. The

Quai d'Orléans, as seen from the Left Bank. Close-up shot of a detail of the same Quai.

48

sectors of a city are, at a certain level, decipherable. But the

Panoramic shot of trees buffeted by a tornado.

personal meaning they have had for us is incommunicable, like

Aerial photograph of the Allée des Cygnes, Paris.

all that clandestinity of private life regarding which we possess
nothing but pitiful documents.

The music dies away.

Official news is elsewhere. The society sends back to itself its

The UN Security Council.   *Khruschev in a room with De Gaulle at his side*

own historical image as a merely superficial and static history

Eisenhower greets De Gaulle.

of its rulers. Those who incarnate the external fatality of what

Patriotic ceremony at the Arc de

is done. The sector of rulers is the very sector of the spectacle.

Triomphe; De Gaulle and Khruschev standing to attention.

The cinema suits them well. Moreover, the cinema everywhere

Eisenhower and the Pope talking.   *Eisenhower in the arms of Franco.*

and with everything it deals with presents exemplary conduct
and heroes modelled on the same old pattern as the rulers.

All existing equilibrium, however, is brought back into question

A riot in the Congo; soldiers disperse the crowd with blows from their rifle butts.

each time unknown people try to live differently. But it's always
far away. We learn of it through papers and news broadcasts.

We remain outside of it, confronted with just another spectacle.

Photo of Djamila Bouhired in a police station. At the edge

We are separated from it by our own non-intervention. It makes

appear the hands of the parachutist-journalist Lartéguy. Tracking shot towards the

us disappointed in ourselves. At what moment was choice

female prisoner's face.

postponed? We have let things go.

I have let time slip away. I have lost what I should have defended.

The young girl talks and laughs.

Couperin: reprise of the March of the Champagne Regiment.

This general critique of separation obviously contains and covers some particulars of memory. A less recognised pain, the awareness of a less explainable indignity. Exactly what separation was it? How quickly we have lived! It is to this point in our unreflecting history that I bring us back.

The music stops.

Everything that concerns the sphere of loss — that is to say, the

In a tracking shot the camera passes quickly across the facade of Saint-Lazare railway

past time I have lost, as well as disappearance, escape, and more

station, then moves away up the Rue du Havre showing numerous cars coming down

generally the flowing past of things, and even what in the

the street.

50

prevalent and therefore most vulgar social sense of the use of time is called wasted time — all this finds in that strangely apt old military expression "*en enfants perdus*" its meeting ground where the sphere of discovery, adventure, *avant-garde*. It is the

A squadron

Sub-title: The new beauty will be of the situation.

crossroads where we have found and lost ourselves.

of the Republican Guard passes by in the distance.

Sub-title: Across the path of all the possible directions which arrive so quickly at this moment, our only friend, our bitter enemy.

All this, it must be admitted, is not clear. It is a completely typical drunken monologue, with its incomprehensible allusions and tiresome delivery. With its vain phrases which do not

March-past of West Point cadets in an equally

await response, and its overbearing explanations. And its silen-

archaic uniform.

ces.

The poverty of means has to express plainly the scandalous

A squad in the course of manouevres.

poverty of the subject.

The events that happen in individual existence as it is organised,

Continuation shot of the movement of the ball in the pinball machine.

Sub-title: Who would wish to have as a friend a man who discourses in such

the events that really concern us and require our participation,

a manner? Who would choose him from amongst others to

are generally precisely those that merit nothing more than our

discuss their affairs? Who would have recourse to him during their

being distant, bored, indifferent spectators. In contrast, the

tribulations? And finally to what useful purpose in life could he be put?

situation that is seen in some artistic transposition is rather often

Mutineers forced back into the court-

attractive, something that would merit our participating in it.

yard of an American prison. The ball disappears.

Sub-title: To disturb everywhere the appearance of the existing false dialogue.

This is a paradox to reverse, to put back on its feet. This is what

Tracking shot over a large number of parked cars.

must be realised in acts. And this idiotic spectacle of the frag-
mented and filtered past, full of sound and fury: it is not a

Sub-title: Already further away than India or China.

question now of transmitting it — of 'rendering' it, as is said —
in another neatly ordered spectacle that would play the game

A couple kiss in the street. Boys and girls at a café table.

Sub-title: A poor rebellion, without language but

of neatly ordered comprehension and participation. No. Any

Two of the

not without a cause. The programme will make itself.   **Sub-title:**

coherent artistic expression already expresses the coherence of

lost children of Saint-Germain-des-Prés.   *A prison guard in a watchtower.*
Partisans of the power of forgetting.

the past, already expresses passivity. It is necessary to destroy

THE SCREEN REMAINS DARK.

Sub-title: Besides, it's less a

memory in art. To destroy the conventions of its communica-
question of form, than of the traces of form, impressions, memories.

tion. To demoralise its fans. What a task! As in blurry, drunken
vision, the memory and language of the film fade out simultaneously. At the extreme, the miserable subjectivity is reversed

Sub-title: We are faced with a world which has fallen apart relentlessly.

into a certain sort of objectivity: a documentary on the conditions of non-communication.

THE SCREEN REMAINS DARK, WITHOUT SUB-
TITLES OR COMMENTARY.

For example, I don't talk about her. False face. False relation-
The young girl who's been featured a lot.

ship. A real person is separated from the interpreter of that
person, if only by the time passed between the event and its

Panoramic shot over cut-up sentences:

Sub-title: The truth of an artifi-

evocation, by a distance that continually increases, that is in-
"The production also shows the mark of youth." "Its terrible, magnificent hopeless

cial society.

53

creasing at this very moment. Just as the conserved expression

disorder."

itself remains separated from those who hear it abstractly and

"All the elements of an American detective novel are there —

without any power over it.

violence, sex, cruelty; but the direction..."

The spectacle in its entirety is the era, an era in which a certain youth has recognised itself, it is the gap between this image and its results; the gap between the vision, the tastes, the refusals

Swimmers filmed

and the projects that previously defined it and the way it has

from under water.   *Photos of a few situ-*

advanced into ordinary life.

ationists.

Couperin: reprise of the March of the Champagne Regiment.

We have invented nothing. We adapt ourselves, with a few

A group at the counter of a cafe.

variations, into the network of possible courses. We get used to it, it seems.

Comic-strip: A man holding a glass thinks: "The dice are cast. Now

Sub-title: How many bottles since then? In how many glasses,

she has to say yes to me, soon, very soon."

in how many bottles has he hidden himself, alone since then?

No one has the enthusiasm on returning from a venture that

Shot of the cover of a detective novel called Swindle. *A woman in profile; further away*

they had on setting out on it. My dears, adventure is dead.

a man, glass in hand.		*A blonde-haired girl.*
Trees in a tornado.	*A napalm explosion.*	*The path cut by the tornado.*
The same blonde girl.	*Panoramic shot over the cut-out sentence: "The wine*	

End of the March.

of life is drunk, and only the dregs are left in this pretentious cellar."

Who will resist? It is necessary to go beyond this partial defeat.

Continuation of the riot in the Congo.

Of course. And how to do it?

Two photos already seen of situationists alternate in and out of shot as the sub-title

Sub-title: It's quite normal that a film on private life should be solely

explains the conversation they are having.

composed of private jokes.

This is a film that interrupts itself and does not come to an end.

The blonde girl.

Sub-title: I didn't undersand it all.

All conclusions remain to be drawn, everything has to be recal-

Asger Jorn.

Sub-title; In the same way one could make a series of documentaries over

culated.

three hours. A kind of 'serial'.

The problem continues to be posed, its expression is becoming more complicated. We have to resort to other measures.

Debord.

Sub-title: The 'Mysteries of New York' of alienation.

Just as there was no profound reason to begin this abstract

Asger Jorn.

Sub-title: Yes, that would be better, more boring; more significant.

message, so there is none for concluding it.

I have scarcely begun to make you understand that I don't

Debord: the camera draws away from him.

Sub-title: More convincing.

intend to play the game.

Sub-title: (To be continued).

What communication have we desired, or experienced, or only simulated?
What true project has been lost?

There remain these endlessly traversed picture postcard landscapes; this
distance organised between each and everyone. Childhood? It's right here;
we've never left it.

In reality no adventure is directly formed for us. The adventures form part of the whole range of legends transmitted by cinema or in other ways; part of the whole spectacular sham of history.

Their divergent emotions neutralise each other and maintain their solid environment of boredom.

These dreams are flashes from the unresolved past. They unilaterally illuminate moments previously lived in confusion and doubt.

Cinema everywhere, and with everything it deals with, presents exemplary conduct and heroes modelled on the same old pattern as the rulers.

Society of the
Spectacle

1973
SIMAR FILMS

This film is dedicated to Alice Becker-Ho.

...an immense accumulation of SPECTACLES. Everything that was directly lived has moved away...

Sequence on Alice.

Subtitle: Since a particular feeling is only one aspect of life, and not life in

Michel Corrette: Sonata in D Major, for cello and harpsichord.

**its entirety, life longs to range across the diversity of feeling, and in so doing
to rediscover itself in the sum of this diversity... In love, the separate still
exists, but no longer as separate: as unified, and the living encounters the
living.**

Board:"This film is dedicated to Alice Becker-Ho."

The entire life of societies in which modern conditions of pro-

The Earth, filmed from a space-rocket, recedes into the distance; an astronaut moves

duction prevail, heralds itself as an immense accumulation of

around in space.

SPECTACLES. Everything that was directly lived has moved away

A long striptease.

into a representation.

The images that detach themselves from every aspect of life fuse
in a common stream where the unity of life can no longer be
re-established. Reality considered PARTIALLY unfolds itself in its
own general unity as a pseudo-world APART, an object of mere
contemplation.

The specialisation of images of the world finds itself accom-

Closed-circuit TV screens in the offices of the Prefecture of Police in Paris, used for

plished in the world of the automised image, where the liar has

the control of the Metro stations and the city streets.

Reality considered PARTIALLY unfolds itself in its own general unity as a pseudo-world APART, an object of mere contemplation.

The spectacle reunites the separate, but reunites it AS SEPARATE.

lied to himself. The spectacle in general, as the concrete inversion of life, is the autonomous movement of the non-living.

The spectacle presents itself simultaneously as society itself, as a part of society, and as INSTRUMENT OF UNIFICATION. As a part

Lee Harvey

of society it is specifically the sector which concentrates all

Oswald passes by surrounded by Dallas police officers; a man rushes forward and

looking and consciousness. Due to the very fact this sector is

shoots him in front of millions of viewers.

SEPARATE, it is the common ground of the deceived gaze and of false consciousness; and the unification it achieves is nothing

A speech by Giscard d'Estaing, the French Prime Minister.

but an official language of generalised separation.

A speech by Servan-Schreiber, communist trade-union bureaucrat.

At the end of May '68 the CGT bureaucrat Séguy tells the Renault workers of the agreements he's just signed at the rue de Grenelle; cynically he says, "At the end of these discussions we accepted what was positive, and made it clear that there was still a lot left to be done". The workers listen in silence.

The spectacle is not an aggregate of images but a social relation

The workers show their anger and contempt.

amongst people, mediated by language. The spectacle, grasped

Fashion show presented by the

in its totality, is both the result and project of the existing mode

designer Courrèges.

of production. It is not a supplement to the real world, its added decoration. It is the heart of the unrealism of the real society. In all its specific forms, as information or propaganda, advertisement or direct entertainment consumption, the spectacle is the present MODEL of socially dominant life. It is the omnipresent affirmation of the choice ALREADY MADE in production and its corollary consumption.

Separation is itself part of the unity of the world, of the global

Workers on the assembly lines in various factories.

social praxis split into image and reality. The social practice before which the autonomous spectacle installs itself is also the real totality which contains the spectacle. But the gash within

Brightly lit shops installed

this totality mutilates it to the point of making the spectacle

on the platforms of the Paris Metro.

appear to be its goal. In a world which is REALLY UPSIDE DOWN,

A girl steps onto a beach.

the true is a moment of the false.

Another girl laying on the beach.

Considered in its own terms, the spectacle is AFFIRMATION of

Nuclear submarines negotiating a sea of ice-floes.

appearance and affirmation of all human life, that is of social life, as mere appearance. But the critique which reaches the truth of the spectacle uncovers it as the visible NEGATION of life; as a negation of life which HAS BECOME VISIBLE.

The spectacle presents itself as something enormously positive,

Fidel Castro speaks to the TV cameras, then to an assembled crowd.

indisputable and inaccessible. It says nothing more than "whatever appears is good, and whatever is good appears". The attitude it requires in principal is this passive acceptance, which in fact it has already obtained by its method of appearing without reply, by its monopoly of appearance.

The spectacle subjugates living men to itself to the extent that

An aircraft carrier aims missiles in all directions, then fires them.

the economy has subjugated them. It is no more than the economy developing itself for itself. It is the faithful reflection of the production of things, and the false objectification of the producers.

Where the real world changes into simple images, the simple

A sequence of aerial bombardments by US forces in Vietnam.

images become real beings and efficient motivations of hypnotic behaviour.

At the rate that necessity is socially dreamed, the dream becomes necessary. The spectacle is the nightmare of enchained modern society which ultimately only expresses its desire to sleep. The spectacle is the guardian angel of this sleep.

The fact that the practical power of modern society has cut itself

Astronauts on the moon with a flag. A spaceman propels himself out of the door of a

loose and built itself an independent empire in the spectacle can

spacecraft remaining attached to a cable.

only be explained by this other fact: that this powerful practice continued to lack cohesion and had remained in contradiction with itself.

The oldest social specialisation, that of power, is at the root of

Beneath the huge dome of the Paris Bourse stockbrokers frenetically carry on their

the spectacle. The spectacle is thus a specialised activity which

business.

speaks for all the others. It is the diplomatic representation of hierarchical society to itself, where all other expression is banned. Here the most modern is also the most archaic.

The generalised cleavage of the spectacle is inseparable from the

The Gardes Mobiles advance.   *A mounted cop repeatedly*

modern STATE, in other words from the general form of cleavage

truncheons a young man sitting on a bench.

within society, a product of the division of social labour and agent of class domination.

In the spectacle, one part of the world REPRESENTS ITSELF to the

Several strippers doing a striptease.

world and is superior to it. The spectacle is nothing but the common language of this separation. What binds the spectators together is no more than an irreversible relation at the very

A couple

centre that maintains their isolation. The spectacle reunites the

stretched out on a bed watching TV.

separate, but reunites it AS SEPARATE.

The worker does not produce himself, he produces an inde-

Immigrant workers at the foot of tower blocks they are constructing in the neighbour-

pendent power. The SUCCESS of this production, its abundance,

hood of La Defense, to the west of Paris; the camera pans up to the summit of their

returns to the producer as an ABUNDANCE OF DISPOSSESSION. The

achievement.

whole time and space of his world becomes FOREIGN to him with the accumulation of his alienated products. The very powers which escaped us SHOW THEMSELVES to us in all their force.

Man separated from his product himself produces, with ever increasing power, all the details of his world; and thus finds himself ever more separated from his world. The more his life is now his product, the more he is separated from his life.

68

The spectacle is CAPITAL to such a degree of accumulation that

The Earth as filmed from the Moon.

it becomes image.

Board: "One could still recognise some cinematographic merit in this film if the rhythm is kept up; but it won't last."

Critical theory must COMMUNICATE itself in its own language. It

During the Russian Civil War a detachment of Red partisans sees a regiment of White

is the language of contradiction, which must be dialectical in

Guards marching towards them, composed of czarist officers serving as simple soldiers.

form as it is in content. It is critique of the totality and historical

Under fire from machine-guns the regiment advances in line, flags flying before them

critique. It is not a 'degree zero of writing' but its reversal. It is

as if on parade.

not a negation of style, but the style of negation.

In its very style, the statement of dialectical theory is a scandal and an abomination in terms of the rules of the dominant language and the taste which they have educated, because in the positive use of existing concepts it simultaneously includes the understanding of their rediscovered FLUIDITY, and their necessary destruction.

The partisans joke about the archaic military style of their adversaries. "What speed!" says one; "Intellectuals!" concludes another.

This style which includes its own critique must express the

Despite losses, the Whites continue to advance in good order and fix bayonets.

domination of the present critique OVER ITS ENTIRE PAST. Through it, the way of stating dialectical theory bears witness to the negative spirit within it. "Truth is not like a product in which one can no longer find any trace of the tool that made it." (Hegel)

This theoretical consciousness of movement within which the very tracts of movement must be present, manifests itself by the REVERSAL of the established relations between concepts and by the *detournement* of all the accomplishments of previous critique.

Ideas improve. The meaning of words participates in the im-

Shaken by the enemy's resolve, a few partisans show signs of hesitation then start to

provement. Plagiarism is necessary. Progress implies it. It hugs

leave the front line.

an author's phrase, makes use of his expression, erases a false idea, and replaces it with a correct one.

The routing partisans run away shouting "Retreat!" and "We're lost!" The Commisar stands himself in front of them and commands: "Halt! Cowards! you've abandoned your comrades. Follow me! Advance!" The partisans take up their positions again.

Detournement is the fluid language of anti-ideology. It appears

The czarist regiment, still in perfectly formed ranks, is about to reach the Red's line

70

within the communication which knows that it cannot pretend

when many of its men are mown down by machine-gun fire.

to guarantee anything definitively and in itself. At its peak, it is the language which cannot be confirmed by any former and supra-critical reference. On the contrary, it is its own coherence, within itself and with applicable facts, which can confirm the old core of truth which it brings out. *Detournement* has not based its cause on anything external to its own truth as present critique.

In theoretical formulation, what openly presents itself as DE-TOURNED, while denying all durable autonomy to the sphere of the theoretically expressed, and bringing about THROUGH THIS VIOLENCE the action that upsets and carries away the entire

Three partisans throw grenades; the White ranks waver. The commanding officer falls;

existing order, is a reminder that this existence of the theoretical

then the standard-bearer; the regiment falls back.

is nothing in itself, and has only to know itself in the light of historical action and the HISTORICAL CORRECTION which is its real truthfulness.

Board: "What the spectacle has taken from reality, it must give back to it. The spectacular expropriators will be expropriated in their turn. The world has already been filmed. Now it is a question of transforming it."

The problem is actually to possess the community of dialogue

'Two ports at sunset' painted by Claude Lorrain.

and the game with time which have been REPRESENTED by poetic-artistic works.

When art becomes independent, represents its world with daz-

Some pretty female faces.

zling colours, a moment of life has grown old and it cannot be rejuvenated with dazzling colours. It can only be evoked in remembrance. The greatness of art only begins to appear at the dusk of life.

Vienna's saloon at night; Johnny Guitar drinks alone. Vienna appears and asks, "Having fun Mr Logan?" Johnny replies, "I couldn't sleep". Vienna: "That stuff help any?" Johnny: "Makes the night go faster. What's keeping you awake?" She: "Dreams, bad dreams." Him: "Yeah, I get 'em sometimes too. Here! This'll chase them away." Vienna refuses the drink: "I've tried that. It didn't seem to help me any." Johnny: "How many men have you forgotten?" She: "As many women as you've remembered." (To the growing accompaniment of the Johnny Guitar *theme.)*

Board: "Therefore, after the direct practice of art has ceased to be the most distinguished thing, and this predicate has been devolved onto theory, such as it is, it detaches itself presently from the latter, in so far as a synthetic post-theoretical practice is formed, which has as its primary goal to be the foundation and the truth of art as philosophy." (August von Czieszkowski, Prolégomènes à l'Historiosophie)

The thought of the social organisation of appearance itself ob-

Marchais, the French Communist Party leader, at an election meeting with the

scured by the generalised SUB-COMMUNICATION which it de-

Socialist Party leader, Mitterand, at his side. They applaud each other. Servan-

fends. It does not know that conflict is at the origin of all things

Schreiber speaks. Marchais on a TV screen.

In its very style, the statement of dialectical theory is a scandal and an abomination in terms of the rules of the dominant language...

When art becomes independent, represents its world with dazzling colours, a moment of life has grown old...

in its world. The specialists of the power of the spectacle, an absolute power within its system of language without answer,

A crowd queueing up to get into a

are absolutely corrupted by their experience of contempt and *cinema.*

the success of contempt; they find their contempt confirmed by the knowledge of the CONTEMPTIBLE MAN whom the spectator really is.

The essential movement of the spectacle consists in absorbing

The camera draws away from a photograph of a naked girl then pans over another.

all that existed in human activity IN A FLUID STATE, in order to possess it in a congealed state, as things that have become exclusive value by their FORMULATION IN THE NEGATIVE of lived value. Through this we recognise our old enemy, THE COM-

President Pompidou visiting a car showroom; he admires

MODITY, which knows so well how to seem at first glance trivial

the latest model which rotates on a pedestal.

and self-evident, while on the contrary it is so complex and full of metaphysical subtleties.

This is the principle of commodity fetishism, the domination of society by 'imperceptible although palpable things', which

A series of pin-up girls in swimming costumes.

reaches its absolute fulfilment in the spectacle, where the world

74

"How many men have you forgotten?" "As many women as you've remembered..."

The specialists of the power of the spectacle, an absolute power within its system of language without answer, are absolutely corrupted by their experience of contempt and the success of contempt.

The essential movement of the spectacle consists in absorbing all that existed in human activity IN A FLUID STATE, in order to possess it in a congealed state, as things...

Every new LIE of advertising is also an AVOWAL of the previous lie.

of the senses is invaded and permeated by a selection of images which at the same time have forced their acknowledgement as the tangible *par excellence*.

The world at once present and absent which the spectacle LETS US SEE is the world of the commodity dominating everything that is lived. And so the world of the commodity is shown FOR WHAT IT IS, because its movement is identical to the growing ESTRANGEMENT of men among themselves and in relation to their global product.

The commodity's domination was at first exerted over the econ-

A factory at Marghera polluting the air around Venice; smoke from factories and cars

omy in an occult manner; the economy itself, the material basis

polluting Mexico City; piles of rubbish outside the church of St-Nicholas-des-Champs

of social life, remained unseen and not understood, like the

in Paris; the filthy waters of the Seine.

familiar which is not necessarily known. In a society where the concrete commodity is rare or in short supply, it is the apparent domination of money which prevents itself as an envoy armed with full powers which speaks in the name of an unknown force. With the industrial revolution, the factory-division of labour and mass-production for the world market, the commodity appears actually as a power that really comes to OCCUPY social life. It is then that political economy takes shape; as the dominant science and the science of domination.

The spectacle is a permanent opium war whose aim is to have

A long sequence on the riots in Watts, Los Angeles, 1965: fires, the forces of order in

the identification of goods with commodities accepted, and of

action, arrests.

satisfaction with survival increasing according to its own laws. But if consumable survival is something which must always increase, this is because it never ceases to INCLUDE DEPRIVATION. If there is nothing beyond increased survival, no point where it might stop its growth, this is not because it is beyond deprivation, but because it is deprivation become enriched. Exchange value could arise only as an agent of use value, but its victory by means of its own weapons created the conditions for its own autonomous domination. Mobilising all human use and seizing the monopoly of its satisfaction, exchange value has ended up DIRECTING USE. The process of exchange became identified with all possible use and reduced use to the mercy of exchange. Exchange value is the *condottiere* of use value, who ends up waging war on his own account.

Use value, which was implicitly included in exchange value, must now be explicitly proclaimed, in the inverted reality of the spectacle, precisely because its factual reality is eroded by the over-developed commodity; and because a pseudo-justification becomes necessary for counterfeit life.

The concentrated result of social labour, at the moment of ECON-

In France a CRS squad being trained in street-fighting.

78

OMIC abundance, becomes visible and subjugates all reality to appearance, which is now its own product. Capital is no longer the visible centre which directs the mode of production: its accumulation spreads it as far as the periphery in the form of tangible objects. The entire expanse of society is its portrait.

The spectacle, like modern society, is simultaneously unified

The CRS continue their manoeuvres: police disguised as radicals line a barricade and

and divided. Like society, it builds its unity on tearing apart. But

hoist a black flag. Their colleagues smartly capture the barricade.

the contradiction, when it emerges in the spectacle, is in turn contradicted by a reversal of its meaning, so that the demonstrated division is unitary, while the demonstrated unity is divided.

The struggle of powers, which have set themselves up for the management of the same socio-economic system, unfurls as an official contradiction, while in fact it is part of the real unity, on a world scale as well in every nation.

At the same time, the spectacular sham struggles of separate

In paternalistic fashion Mao Tse-Tung receives President Nixon in Beijing.

power's rival forms are real in that they translate the unequal and antagonistic development of the system, the relatively contradictory interests of classes or their sub-divisions which acknowledge the system and define their own participation in its power. These different oppositions can pass themselves off in the spectacle, according to completely different criteria, as absolutely distinct forms of society. But in terms of the actual reality of their specific sectors, the truth of their particularity is in the universal system which contains them, the unique movement which has made the planet its field: capitalism.

The movement of BANALISATION, under the shimmering diver-

In Vietnam helicopters machine-gun anything on the ground that moves.

sions of the spectacle, dominates modern society the world over and at every point where the developed consumption of commodities has multiplied, on the level of appearance, the roles and objects to chose from. The relics of religion and the family

A priest blesses a British submarine.

(which remain the chief form of the heritage of class power) — and the moral repression which they assure — can merge with the repeated affirmation of an enjoyment of THIS world; this

An urban traffic jam:

world only being produced precisely as a pseudo-enjoyment

in vain do the cars try to move.

maintaining repression within it. The smug acceptance of what exists can also merge with purely spectacular rebellion: this is

Johnny Halliday sings and the audience scream

the manifestation of the simple fact that dissatisfaction itself

with delight; the singer rolls on the ground.

became a commodity as soon as economic abundance was in a

position to extend its production to the treatment of such a raw material.

By concentrating in himself or herself the image of a popular role, the celebrity, spectacular representation of a living human being, concentrates this banality. The condition of the 'Star' is the specialisation of the APPARENTLY LIVED; the object of ident-

The Beatles descending

ification with shallow apparent life, which must compensate for

from an aeroplane are welcomed by teenage girls; cameras flash. Eddy Mitchell sings,

the fragments of actually lived productive specialisations. Cele-

to general applause; Dick Rivers sings.

brities exist in order to represent various types of life-styles and styles of comprehending society, free to express themselves GLOBALLY. They incarnate the inaccessible result of social LA-

Marilyn Monroe seen in her last (unfinished) film.

BOUR by miming the sub-products of this labour, which are magically projected above it as its goal: POWER and HOLIDAYS, decision and consumption, which are at the beginning and the end of an undiscussed process. On the one hand governmental

François Mitterand.

power personalises itself in a pseudo-celebrity, on the other, the star of consumption gets itself elected by plebiscite as a pseudo-

Several shots of Marilyn Monroe.

power over the lived. But just as the activities of the star are not really global, so they are not really varied.

81

It is the UNITY OF MISERY which hides under the spectacular

German workers leaving a factory shortly after Hitler's rise to power; underground

oppositions. If various forms of the same alienation fight each

leaflets are thrown to them from a skylight; the workers pick them up and start to read.

other behind the masks of total choice, it is because they are all
erected upon real contradictions that are repressed. The spec-

A convoy of police vans bring up the CRS.

tacle exists in a CONCENTRATED or DIFFUSED form depending on
the necessities of the particular stage of misery which it denies
and supports. In both cases, it is the same image of happy

In Vietnam, US troops comb the fields for VC; prisoners are taken.

unification surrounded by desolation and horror, in the tranquil
centre of unhappiness.

The concentrated spectacle belongs essentially to bureaucratic

The camera follows Hitler as he walks along the ranks of his followers, then mounts a

capitalism, even though it can be imported as a technique of

huge platform.

state power over more backward, mixed economies, or at certain
moments of crisis advanced capitalism. Actually, bureaucratic

Brezhnev, the Russian Presi-

property is itself concentrated in such a way that the individual

dent, and other high bureaucrats on a platform in Moscow; their subjects march before

bureaucrat relates only by way of the bureaucratic community,

them.

82

only as a member of this community, to the ownership of the global economy. Moreover, the production of commodities,

During a NATO exercise a large tank manoeuvres demon-

which is less developed, also presents itself in concentrated

strating all its possible uses.

form: the commodity the bureaucracy retains is the whole of social labour, and what it sells in return to society is its survival *en bloc*. The dictatorship of the bureaucratic economy cannot leave to the exploited masses any considerable margin of choice, since this economy had to choose everything by itself, and since any other choice, outside of it, whether it concerns food or music, thus already embodies the choice of the complete destruction of the bureaucracy.

The diffuse spectacle accompanies the abundance of com-

Lines of cars in a traffic jam; spectacularly presented food; an old painting; modern

modities, the undisturbed development of modern capitalism.

furnishing; exotic women in cages; a train arriving at a Metro station.

Here, every single commodity is justified in the name of the grandeur of the production of the totality of the objects of which the spectacle is an apologetic catalogue.

Irreconcilable assertions crowd onto the scene of the unified spectacle of the economy of abundance, just as different star-commodities simultaneously support contradictory projects for the provisioning of society: the spectacle of automobiles wants a perfect traffic system which destroys the old cities, while the

Disintegrat-

spectacle of the city itself needs museum areas. Therefore, the

ing statues on the roof of a Venetian church.   *Two Tahitian*

already problematic satisfaction reputedly linked to the CON-

women on a sailing boat.

SUMPTION OF THE WHOLE, is immediately falsified, inasmuch as

The camera pans across a typical modern living-room,

the real consumer can directly touch only a succession of frag-

homing in on the TV which is the room's focal point.

ments of this commodity happiness – fragments from which every time the quality attributed to the whole is obviously missing.

Every given commodity fights for itself, cannot acknowledge

A series of pin-up girls, naked or with very little clothing.

the others, and attempts to impose itself everywhere as if it were the only one. The spectacle then, is the epic poem of this struggle, an epic which cannot be concluded by the fall of any Troy. The spectacle does not sing the praises of men and their weapons, but of commodities and their passions. In this blind struggle, every commodity pursuing its passion unconsciously realises something higher: the becoming-world of the commodity, which is also the becoming-commodity of the world. So, by a TRICK OF COMMODITY LOGIC, what is SPECIFIC in the commodity

84

wears itself out in the fight while the commodity-form moves towards its absolute realisation.

In the image of the society happily unified by consumption, real division is only SUSPENDED until the next non-accomplishment in the consumable. Each specific product which represents hope

The latest models of various cars are presented to an enthusiastic

for a dazzling short-cut to the promised land of total consump-

crowd.

tion, is ceremoniously presented in its turn as the decisive entity. But as in the case of the simultaneous diffusion of seemingly aristocratic first-names carried by almost all individuals of the same age, the objects from which one expects a unique power could not have been proposed for the devotion of the masses unless it had been produced in large enough numbers to be consumed massively. A product acquires prestige only when it is placed at the centre of social life as the revealed mystery of the ultimate goal of production.

The object which was prestigious in the spectacle becomes

Industrial manufacture of cream-cakes, following the mechanisation of confectionery.

vulgar as soon as it enters into the home of the consumer, and at the same time that it enters the home of all the others. Too late, it reveals its essential poverty, which it naturally gets from the misery of its production. But, by then, another object already carries the justification of the system and the demand to be recognised.

The fraud of satisfaction must denounce itself by being replaced,

Racing cars speeding round a race-track.

following the change of products and the general conditions of production. That which asserted its definitive excellence with perfect impudence nevertheless changes, both in the diffuse and in the concentrated spectacle, and it is the system alone which must continue. Stalin, as well as the outmoded commodity are denounced precisely by those who imposed them. Every NEW LIE of advertising is also an AVOWAL of the previous lie. The fall

Mao Tse-Tung with Lin Piao.

of every figure of totalitarian power reveals the ILLUSORY COM-

Stalin on a platform applauded by a

MUNITY which approved him unanimously, and was no more

Party Congress; people marching in Red Square: a huge portrait of Lenin can be seen.

than an agglomeration of solitudes without illusions.

What the spectacle offers as eternal is based on change, and must

In Budapest insurrectionary workers demolish a giant statue of Stalin: only his boots

change with its base. The spectacle is absolutely dogmatic and

are left.

at the same time cannot really arrive at any solid dogma. Nothing stops for it; this condition is natural to it yet most contrary

The camera pans across a woman up to her smiling face.

to its inclination.

The unreal unity proclaimed by the spectacle masks the class

Sequence on the activity in a packing factory.

division on which the real unity of the capitalist mode of production rests. What obliges the producers to participate in the construction of the world is also what separates them from it. What brings together men liberated from their local and national boundaries is also what pulls them apart. What requires a more profound rationality is also what nourishes the irrationality of hierarchical exploitation and repression. What creates the abstract power of society creates its concrete UNFREEDOM.

Close up of Durruti, the Spanish Anarchist leader: Board: "Are we really living

Michel Corrette: Sonata in D Major, for cello and harpsichord.

proletarians, are we really living? This age that we count on, and where everything we count on is no longer ours, can it be called a life? And can't we recognise how much we keep losing as the years pass by?" Close-up of a revolutionary sailor from Eisenstein's October, he shakes his head negatively. Durruti looks at him. The sailor repeats his negative gesture. Board: "Rest and food, aren't they feeble remedies for the continual illness that belabours us? And this other thing that we call and is well known as the final illness, what more is it than a sudden attack of the last of the evil that we bring with us into the world at birth?" The Petrograd sailor agrees.

The music fades away.

Capitalist production has unified space, which is no longer

Battleships on the high seas. French, then English Marines disembark in Shanghai.

limited by external societies. This unification is at the same time

An American soldier checks the Chinese passers-by; French soldiers push back the

an extensive and intensive process of BANALISATION. The accu-

crowd; English soldiers on patrol; the barbed wire which marks the front of the

mulation of mass-produced commodities produced for the ab-

Concession guarded by French colonial infantry.

stract space of the the market, had to break down all regional and local barriers and all the corporative restrictions of the Middle Ages that preserved the QUALITY of craft production, and had also to destroy the autonomy and quality of places. This power of homogenisation is the heavy artillery which battered down all Chinese walls.

In order to become ever more identical to itself, to get as close as possible to motionless monotony, THE FREE SPACE OF THE COMMODITY is henceforth constantly modified and reconstructed.

The society which eliminates geographical distance recovers

British soldiers closing a gate into the Concession.

distance internally as spectacular separation.

Tourism, human circulation considered as consumption, a by-

Tourists visiting Paris aboard the 'bateaux mouches' on the River Seine; guides give

product of the circulation of commodities, is fundamentally

commentaries on the sights to be seen.

nothing more than the leisure of going to see what has become banal. The economic organisation of visits to different places is already in itself the guarantee of their EQUIVALENCE. The same modernisation that removed time from travel also removed from it the reality of space.

Board: "A society based on the expansion of alienated industrial labour naturally becomes thoroughly unhealthy, noisy, ugly and dirty, just like a factory."

The society which moulds its entire surroundings has de-

A large agglomeration of modern architecture.

veloped a special technique for shaping its very territory, the solid ground of this collection of tasks. Urbanism is the seizure of the natural and human environment by capitalism, which developing logically into absolute domination, can and must now remake the totality of space as ITS OWN SETTING.

Board: "Man goes back to living in caves but... the worker continues to occupy them only precariously, it being for him an alien habitation which can be withdrawn from him any day, a place from which if he does not pay, he can be thrown out any day. For this house of death he must pay." (Marx, Manuscripts of 1844)

If all the technical forces of capitalism must be understood as

CRS riot police at the ready on their chosen terrain.

tools for the making of separations, in the case of urbanism we are dealing with the equipment at the basis of these technical forces, with the treatment of the ground that suits their deployment, with the very technique OF SEPARATION.

For the first time a new architecture, which in all previous

Models of recent architecture for holiday resorts, either next to the sea as 'marinas' or

epochs had been reserved for the satisfaction of the ruling

in the mountains; views of the real thing.

For the first time, a new architecture, which in all previous epochs had been reserved for the satisfaction of the ruling classes, is directly aimed AT THE POOR.

History, which threatens this twilight world, is also the force which could subject space to lived time.

classes, is directly aimed AT THE POOR. The formal poverty and
the gigantic spread of this new living experience both come from
its MASS character, which is implicit in its purpose and in modern conditions of construction. The threshold crossed by the
growth of society's material power, and the LAG in the conscious
domination of this power, are clearly shown in urbanism.

Board: *"The environment, always being reconstructed more hurriedly for reasons of
profit and repressive control, becomes at the same time more fragile and incites
vandalism. In its spectacular period, capitalism rebuilds everything AS JUNK and
produces those who will burn it down. So its decor becomes everywhere as inflammable
as a French school."*

History, which threatens this twilight world, is also the force
The cruiser Aurora *proceeds up the River Neva just before dawn; as day breaks it sets*
which could subject space to lived time. Proletarian revolution
down a company of sailors onto the shore.

is the CRITIQUE OF HUMAN GEOGRAPHY through which individuals and communities have to create places and events related
The Tower of Babel.

to the appropriation, no longer just of their labour, but of their
total history. In this game's changing space, and in the freely
A landscape painting by an early Italian master.

chosen variations in the game's rules, the autonomy of place can
be rediscovered without the reintroduction of an exclusive at-
tachment to the land, thus bringing back the reality of travel,
and of life considered as a journey which contains its entire
meaning within itself.

In Nick Ray's film Johnny Guitar *the hero is seen riding through a sand-storm across a typical 'Western' landscape. Johnny arrives in front of a grand saloon standing completely isolated in the wilderness. He goes in. There are no customers but two croupiers stand at the roulette tables idly spinning the roulette wheels. Johnny saunters up to the bar and orders a drink.* CUT TO: *a scene from Josef von Sternberg's film* Shanghai Gesture; *a European man is showing a young girl round the casino, describing those present: "Javanese, Hindus, Chinese, Portuguese, Filipinos, Russians, Malays... what a party!" The young girl says, "If I was recognised, what a fuss there'd be! Compared to such an evil place as this, the rest of the world is like a children's playground. I would have thought such a place possible only in a dream. I feel like I'm dreaming; anything might happen here, at any moment".*

The time of production, commodity-time, is an infinite accumu-

Workers in a tyre factory.

lation of equivalent intervals. It is the abstraction of irreversible time, all of whose segments must prove on the chronometer their merely quantitative equality. This time is in reality exactly what is in its EXCHANGEABLE character.

The general time of human non-development also exists in the

Long sequence on a holiday crowd in St-Tropez.

complementary form of CONSUMABLE TIME which returns to the daily life of society based on this determined production, as PSEUDO-CYCLICAL TIME.

Pseudo-cyclical time is the time of consumption of modern economic survival, of increased survival, where daily life continues to be deprived of decision and remains bound, no longer to the natural order, but to the pseudo-nature developed in alienated labour; and so this time QUITE NATURALLY reestab-

92

lishes the ancient cyclical rhythm which regulated the survival of pre-industrial societies. Pseudo-cyclical time leans on the natural remains of cyclical time and also uses it to compose new homologous combinations: day and night, work and rest, the recurrence of holidays.

Consumable pseudo-cyclical time is spectacular time, both at the time of consumption of images in the narrow sense, and as the image of consumption of time in the broad sense. The time

Couples sit-

of image consumption, the medium of all commodities, is insep-

ting in front of their TV and Hi-Fi systems.

arably the field where the instruments of the spectacle exert themselves fully, and also their goal, the location and main form of all specific consumption.

The social image of the consumption of time, in turn, is exclu-

Crowd in St-Tropez; topless women walking along.

sively dominated by moments of leisure and vacation, moments presented AT A DISTANCE and desirable by definition, like every spectacular commodity. Here this commodity is explicitly presented as the moment of real life, and the point is to wait for its cyclical return. But even in those very moments reserved for living, it is still the spectacle that is to be seen and reproduced, becoming ever more intense. What was represented as genuine life reveals itself simply as more GENUINELY SPECTACULAR life.

...individuals and communities have to create places and events related to the appropriation, no longer just of their labour, but of their total history.

The ocial image of the consumption of time, in turn, is exclusively dominated by moments of leisure and vacation, moments presented AT A DISTANCE and desirable by definition...

94

While the consumption of cyclical time in ancient societies was

Planes take off from an aircraft carrier and return again.

consistent with the real labour of those societies, the pseudo-cyclical consumption of the developed economy is in contradiction with the abstract irreversible time of its production. While cyclical time was the time of immobile illusion really lived, spectacular time is the time of self-changing reality, lived in illusion.

What is constantly new in the process of production of things is not found in consumption, which remains the expanded repetition of the same. In spectacular time, since dead labour continues to dominate living labour, the past dominates the present.

Another side of the deficiency of general historical life is that

Lovers, as though from memory.

individual life as yet has no history. The pseudo-events which rush by in spectacular dramatisations have not been by those informed of them; moreover they are lost in the inflation of their hurried replacement at every throb of the spectacular machinery. Furthermore, what is really lived has no relation to the official irreversible time as society and is in direct opposition to the pseudo-cyclical rhythm of the consumable by-product of this time. This individual experience of separate daily life remains without language, without concept, without critical access to its own past, which has been recorded nowhere. It is not communicated. It is not understood and is forgotten to the profit of the false spectacular memory of the unmemorable.

At the bar of the saloon a certain tension reigns between Johnny Guitar, the proprietress Vienna, and her lover, Dancing Kid. Vienna speaks to the Kid: "That's the way it goes, lose one, find one." Turning to Johnny she says, "Play something for me Mr Guitar". Johnny asks, "Anything special?" Vienna: "Just put a lot of love in." Dancing Kid shouts: "He ain't gonna play so good all stretched out on that crap table." Untroubled, Johnny quips, "What's eating the fancy man?" Vienna: "I don't know. What's the trouble kid?" The Kid replies angrily, "I'm in no trouble, he is. Fooling with a strange woman can bring a man a lot of grief". Johnny asks Vienna, "Are you a strange woman?" She replies: "Only to strangers." Dancing Kid, indignantly: "What's going on with you two?" Johnny replies cockily, "Just what you see friend". The Kid: "Oh you picked the wrong place to come to mister!" Johnny looks him in the eyes: "The lady sent for me, not you." Dancing Kid produces a coin: "Heads I'm going to kill you mister. Tails you play her a tune." He flips the coin. Vienna plucks it from the air and asks Johnny to play something. He starts to strum the Johnny Guitar theme. Vienna listens dreamily for a minute them stops him and says drily, "Play something else".

The spectacle, as the present social organisation of the paralysis

A Francoist cavalry patrol followed by a whole squadron slowly pass right under the

of history and memory, of the abandonment of history built on

nose of the partisans' machine-gun, which they have failed to notice concealed in the

the foundation of historical time, is FALSE CONSCIOUSNESS OF

sierra. (For Whom the Bell Tolls)

TIME.

Beneath the visible FASHIONS which disappear and reappear on the trivial surface of contemplated pseudo-cyclical time, the GRAND STYLE of the age is always located in what is orientated by the obvious and secret necessity of revolution.

In the Winter Palace, soon to be attacked, a little owl inside an automatic clock turns its head. Board: "It was nearing midnight." Once more the owl turns its head.

Michel Corrette: Sonata in D Major, for

Cello and harpsichord

Debord

Subtitle: Therefore, since I cannot be the lover who could seduce these glib-tongued times, I am determined to be instead the wicked spoil-sport of these frivolous days.

The music fades away

In the bar of the Shanghai Gesture, an old Chinaman presents Dr Omar, in arab dress, to a young girl: "This is my very best friend, Omar." After a short while the Chinaman moves away. The young girl enquires, "Are you an Egyptian? A businessman?" Dr Omar replies, "No, a doctor — Dr Omar of Shanghai and Gomorrha". The girl: "Any relation to Omar the poet? A book of verses underneath the bough..." He continues, "A pitcher of wine, a loaf of bread, and you beside me singing in the wilderness". She: "Doctor of what in fact?" He replies urbanely: "Doctor of nothing, Miss Smith. It sounds impressive and hurts no one, unlike most doctors." The girl: "And your burnous, is it real? Where were you born?" He confides, "I was born under a full moon on the sands near Damascus. My father was an Armenian merchant. As for my mother, the less said about her the better; half French, the other half lost in the mists of time. I am a thoroughbred mongrel. I'm related to all the Earth and to everything human". Smiling, she says, "Explain to me then our friend's disappearance". Omar replies, "We were alone since I first saw you". The camera pans over an astronomical map entitled 'The Revolution of the Earth'.

Reasoning about history is inseparably REASONING ABOUT *Machiavelli.*

POWER. Greece was the moment when power and its change

Detail of 'The Battle of San Romano' by Uccello.

were discussed and understood: the DEMOCRACY OF THE MAS-
TERS of society. Greek conditions were the inverse of the conditions known to the despotic State; where power settles its

Brezhnev and other leading bureaucrats on a platform

accounts only with itself within the inaccessable obscurity of its

in Moscow, alogside Red Army marshals.

densest point: through PALACE REVOLUTION, which is placed
beyond the pale of discussion by success or failure alike.

Board: "In the Chronicle of the North, *men act in silence; they make war, they
conclude peace, but they themselves don't say (and the* Chronicle *doesn't add
anything more) why they make war or for what reasons they make peace; in the city
or at the court of the prince, there is nothing to be heard, all is silent; they all assemble
behind closed doors and deliberate amongst themselves; the doors open and men come
out and appear on stage; there, they carry out some form of action, but they act in
silence." (Soloviev,* A History of Russia from Ancient Times*)*

The dry unexplained chronology of divine power speaking to

On the poop deck of the Battleship Potemkin the firing squad refuse to execute their

its servants, which wants to be understood only as the earthly

comrades; in a theatre English schoolchildren make gestures showing their strong

execution of the commandments of myth, can be surmounted

approval.

and become conscious history; this requires that real participation in history be lived by extended groups. Out of this practical
communication among those who RECOGNISED EACH OTHER as
possessors of a singular present, who experienced the qualitative richness of events as their activity and as the place where

they lived – their epoch – arises the general language of histori-

A regiment of cavalry draw their sabres prior to

cal communication. Those for whom irreversible time has

charging.

existed discover within it the MEMORABLE as well as the MENACE
OF FORGETTING: "Herodotus of Halicarnassus here presents the

Revolutionary assemblies in occupied buildings, 1968.

results of his study, so that time may not abolish the works of
men..."

General Sheridan, on horseback, enters a frontier fort where several of his squadrons are stationed. He is welcomed by a colonel who has served under his command in the Civil War. The General briefs him on a hazardous operation against the Indians and concludes, "If you fail, I can assure you that that the court-martial that will judge you will be composed of our old comrades from the Shenandoah. I will choose them myself". The old colonel, lost in thought, says only, "The Shenandoah...". And the General, reminiscing, adds, "I wonder what the historians will write one day about the Shenandoah".

The victory of the bourgeoisie is the victory of PROFOUNDLY

The 'Tennis Court Oath' during the French Revolution, 1789.

HISTORICAL time, because this is the time of economic production which transforms society continuously and from top to
bottom. So long as agrarian production remains the principal

A ceremonial meal in the Shanghai Concession.

activity, the cyclical time which remains at the base of society
nourishes the coalesced forces of TRADITION which fetter all
movement. But the irreversible time of the bourgeois economy
eradicates these vestiges on every corner of the globe. History,

which until then had seemed to be only the movement of individuals of the ruling class, and thus was the history of events, is now understood as the GENERAL MOVEMENT, and in

Stockbrokers busily engaged at the Paris Bourse.

this relentless movement, individuals are sacrificed. This history which discovers its foundation in political economy now knows of the existence of what had been its unconscious, but it nevertheless remains the unconscious which it cannot bring to the light of day. It is only this blind prehistory, a new fatality dominated by no-one, that the commodity economy has democratised. Thus the bourgeoisie made known to society and

Recent street-battles in Holland, Ireland and England.

imposed upon it an irreversible historical time, but kept its USE from society. "There was history, but there is no more", because the class of owners of the economy, which cannot break with ECONOMIC HISTORY, is directly threatened by all other irreversible use of time and must repress it. The ruling class, made up of SPECIALISTS IN THE POSSESSION OF THINGS who are themselves therefore a possession of things, must link its fate with the preservation of this reified history, with the permanence of a new immobility WITHIN HISTORY. For the first time the worker at the base of society, is not materially a STRANGER TO HISTORY, because it is the base that irreversibly moves society. In the demand to LIVE the historical time which it makes, the proletariat finds the simple unforgettable centre of its revolutionary project; and every attempt (thwarted until now) to realise this project marks a point of possible departure for new historical life.

With the development of capitalism, irreversible time is UNIFIED
Three black girls dancing.

ON A WORLD SCALE. Universal history becomes a reality because the entire world is gathered under the development of this time. But this history, which is everywhere simultaneously the same, is still only a refusal within history of history itself. What appears the world over as the SAME DAY is the time of economic production cut up into equal abstract fragments. Unified irreversible time is the time of the WORLD MARKET and, as a corollary, of the world spectacle.

The irreversible time of production is first of all the measure of
A hovercraft on the sea; an airport with a plane taking off.

commodities. Therefore the time officially affirmed over the entire expanse of the globe as the GENERAL TIME OF SOCIETY, refers only to the specialised interests which constitute it and is NO MORE THAN A PARTICULAR TIME. The class struggles of the

The Earth's rotation, filmed from

long REVOLUTIONARY EPOCH inaugurated by the rise of the
space.

bourgeoisie, develop together with the THOUGHT OF HISTORY, the dialectic, the thought which no longer stops to look for the meaning of what is, but rises to a knowledge of the dissolution of all that is, and in its movement dissolves all separation.

This historical thought is as yet only the consciousness which always arrives too late, and which pronounces the justification *post festum.* Thus it has gone beyond separation only IN THOUGHT. The paradox which consists of making the meaning of all reality depend on its historical completion, and at the same time of revealing this meaning as it makes itself the completion of history, flows from the simple fact that the thinker of the

Hegel.

bourgeois revolutions of the seventeenth and eighteenth centuries sought in his philosophy only a RECONCILIATION with the results of these revolutions.

Under fire from artillery, a detachment of Kronstadt sailors attack with fixed bayonets, while singing 'The International'.

When the proletariat demonstrates by its own existence,

The proletariat during the revolutionary days in Barcelona, 1936, and in Petrograd,

through acts, that this thought of history is not forgotten, the

1917.

denial of the CONCLUSION is at the same time the confirmation of the method.

The shortcomings of Marx's theory is the shortcoming of the

A long battle in the American Civil War.

revolutionary struggle of the proletariat of his time. The working class did not set off the permanent revolution in the Germany of 1848; the Commune was defeated in isolation. Revolutionary theory thus cannot yet achieve its own total existence.

102

All the theoretical insufficiency of the SCIENTIFIC defence of the proletarian revolution, in terms of content as well as form of

A map of the

exposition, can be traced to an identification of the proletariat

Winter Palace in Petrograd on which the lines of attack have been pencilled in.

with the bourgeoisie FROM THE STANDPOINT OF THE REVOL-

A map of the Tuileries Palace in the Paris of 1792.

UTIONARY SEIZURE OF POWER.

In the Spanish Civil War, a partisan who has made it through the lines brings a last-minute warning that the Francoists have been alerted to the imminent republican offensive and await them in force. General Golz, a Russian officer in the service of the Republic, speaks on the telephone from a dug-out at the front. He watches a wave of bombers fly over, heralding the start of the offensive, and replies, "Too late. That means we're done for. This time we fail. Too bad. Yes, too bad".

The only two classes which effectively correspond to Marx's

Continuation of the same battle in the American Civil War.

theory, the two pure classes towards which the entire analysis of CAPITAL leads, the bourgeoisie and the proletariat, are also the only two revolutionary classes in history, but in very different conditions: the bourgeois revolution is over; the proletarian revolution is a project born of the foundation of the preceding revolution but differing from it qualitatively. By neglecting the ORIGINALITY of the historical role of the bourgeoisie, one masks the concrete originality of the proletarian project, which can attain nothing unless it carries its own banners and knows the 'immensity of its tasks'. The bourgeoisie came to power because it is the class of the developing economy. The proletariat cannot itself come to power except by becoming the CLASS OF CON-SCIOUSNESS. The growth of productive forces cannot guarantee such power, even by way of increasing dispossession which it brings about. A Jacobin seizure of power cannot be its instrument. No IDEOLOGY can help the proletariat disguise its goals as general goals, because the proletariat cannot preserve any partial reality which is really its own.

This ideological estrangement from theory can no longer then

Kronstadt sailors victoriously follow-up their attack.

recognise the practical verification of unitary historical thought which it betrayed when such verification emerges in the spontaneous struggle of the workers; all it can do is repress every manifestation and memory of such verification. Yet these historical forms which appeared in struggle are precisely the practical milieu which the theory needed in order to be true. They

The Winter Palace being stormed.

are requirements of the theory which have not been formulated theoretically. The SOVIET was not a theoretical discovery, yet its existence in practice was already the highest truth of the International Workingmen's Association.

The Vendome column which has been pulled down.   Marx.

Subtitle: You will find out

Michel Corrette: Sonata in D Major, for cello and harpsichord.

how bitter is the taste of foreign bread, and how arduous is the path when

Bakunin.

climbing or descending foreign stairways. And the heaviest burden that you will drag with you will be the unpleasant and foolish company with whom you shall fall into the valley of exile. But afterwards what will be to your credit will be that it was your decision, and yours alone.

The same historical moment when Bolshevism triumphed FOR

A Red Army parade: the infantry.

ITSELF in Russia, and Social-Democracy fought victoriously FOR THE OLD WORLD, marks the inauguration of the state of affairs which is at the heart of the domination of the modern spectactle: WORKING-CLASS REPRESENTATION radically opposed itself to

Trotsky.

the working-class.

Board: "Those who want to set up state capitalism as a totalitarian bureaucracy without overthrowing the Councils, or those who want to abolish class society without condemning all the Unions and the specialised hierarchical parties — they will only last a short while."

The Stalinist epoch reveals the reality behind the BUREAU-

The rest of the Red Army: tanks, artillery and rockets.

CRACY: it is the continuation of the power of the economy and the preservation of the essence of the market society — commodity labour. It is the proof of the independent economy, which dominates society to the point of recreating for its own ends the class domination which is necessary to it. In other words, the bourgeoisie has created an autonomous power which, so long as its autonomy lasts, can even do without a bourgeoisie. The totalitarian bureaucracy is not 'the last owning

On the Odessa steps

class in history' in the sense of Bruno Rizzi, it is only a SUB-

in 1905 czarist troops open fire on a crowd of demonstrators.

STITUTE RULING CLASS for the commodity economy. Capitalist private property in decline is replaced by a simplified, less diversified surrogate which is CONDENSED as the collective property of the bureaucratic class. This under-developed ruling-class is the expression of economic under-development, and has no perspective other than to overcome the retardation of this development in certain regions of the world. It was the workers' party organised according to the bourgeois model of separation which furnished the hierarchical-statist cadre for this supplementary edition of the ruling-class.

The totalitarian-ideological class in power is the power of an

A meeting of the French 'United Left': the Stalinists and their allies on a platform and

upside-down world: the stronger it is, the more it claims not to

in the meeting hall; a speech by Mitterand; a speech by Marchais.

exist, and its force serves above all to affirm its non-existence. It is modest only on this point because its official non-existence must also coincide with the *nec plus ultra* of historical development, which must at the same time be attributed to its infallible command. Extended everywhere, the bureaucracy must be the CLASS INVISIBLE to consciousness: as a result, all social life becomes insane. The social organisation of the absolute lie flows from this fundamental contradiction.

"Slaves, arise! Arise! The world will change from below."

A new epoch has begun. After the workers' first attempts at subversion, IT IS CAPITALIST ABUNDANCE WHICH HAS FAILED.

Board: "The higher up one goes in this bureaucracy of the intellect, the more one encounters the most ludicrous brains." (Marx, Remarks on the recent implementation of the Prussian censorship)

Stalinism was the reign of terror within the bureaucratic class

Brezhnev and other stalinist bureaucrats receiving flowers; the union bosses in the

itself. The terrorism at the base of this class's power must also

Renault factory. Renault workers in 1968, locked inside the factory by the unions,

strike this class because it possesses no juridical guarantee, no

watch some naive leftist demonstrators pass by in turn surrounded by their own

recognised existence as an owning class, which it could extend

bureaucrats.

to every one of its members. Its real property being hidden, the bureaucracy became proprietor by way of false consciousness. False consciousness can maintain its absolute power only by means of absolute terror, where all real motives are ultimately lost. The members of the bureaucratic class in power have a right of ownership over society only collectively, as participants

Stalin speaks at

in a fundamental lie: they have to play the role of the proletariat

length.

leading a socialist society, they have to be actors loyal to a script of ideological disloyalty. But effective participation in this falsehood requires that it be recognised as actual participation. No bureaucrat can support his right to power individually, since proving that he's a proletarian socialist would mean presenting himself as the opposite of a bureaucrat, and proving that he's a bureaucrat is impossible since the official truth of the bureau-

108

cracy is that it does not exist. Hence every bureaucrat depends absolutely on the CENTRAL GUARANTEE of the ideology which recognises the collective participation in its 'socialist power' of ALL THE BUREAUCRATS IT DOES NOT ANNIHILATE. If all the bureaucrats taken together decide everything, the cohesion of their own class can be assured only by the concentration of their terrorist power in a single person. In this person resides the only practical truth of falsehood IN POWER: the indiputable permanence of its constantly adjusted frontier. Stalin decides without appeal who is ultimately to be a possessing bureaucrat – in other words who should be named a 'proletarian in power' and who a 'traitor in the pay of the Mikado and Wall Street'. The bureaucratic atoms find the common essence of their right only in the person of Stalin. Stalin is the world sovereign who in this manner knows himself as the absolute person for whose consciousness there is no higher spirit. "The sovereign of the world has effective consciousness of what he is — the universal power of efficacy — in the destructive violence which he asserts against the Self of his subjects, the contrasting Others." Just as he is the power that defines the terrain of domination, he is "THE POWER WHICH RAVAGES THIS TERRAIN ".

As the Reichstag burns, the Hamburg communists hold their last meeting. A militant denounces this provocation by the Nazi government, and realising that they intend to ban the Communist Party declares, "Hitler equals War", at a time when the moment for civil war has already passed. A police officer present announces that the meeting is over. The security police burst into the room and begin beating up those present who have begun to sing 'The Internationale'.

A picture of a Nazi officer. General Franco. *German tanks in action; officers of the*

Subtitle: There is a valley in

Abraham Lincoln Column of the International Brigade.

Spain called Jamara. It is a place that all of us know only too well. It is there that we lost our youth, as well as the greater part of our old age.

Spanish partisans, pursued by Francoist soldiers, defend themselves on top of their last hill. An assembly of political prisoners in a German concentration camp. Somewhere around Paris a crowd watch a little girl spinning a roundabout. The Place de la Concorde lit up at night. The rooftops of Paris. Board: "Social peace, re-established with such great difficulty, had only lasted a few years when, to herald its end, there appeared those who will enter the annals of crime under the name 'situationists'.

When the proletariat discovers that its own externalised power

Barricades in May '68; fires and fighting in the night.

collaborates in the constant reinforcement of capitalist society, not only in the form of its labour, but also in the form of unions, parties, or the state power it has built to emancipate itself, it also discovers from concrete historical experience that it is the class totally opposed to all congealed externalisation and all specialisation of power. It carries the REVOLUTION WHICH CANNOT LET ANYTHING REMAIN OUTSIDE OF ITSELF, the demand for the permanent domination of the present over the past, and the total critique of separation. And that is what must find its suitable form in action. No quantitative amelioration of its misery, no illusion of hierarchic integration is a lasting solution for its dissatisfaction, because the proletariat cannot truly recognise itself in a particular wrong it suffered, nor IN THE RIGHTING OF A PARTICULAR WRONG. It cannot recognise itself in the righting

of a large number of wrongs either, but only in the ABSOLUTE
WRONG of being relegated to the margin of life.

Rue Gay-Lussac at dawn. The rostrum of the mass-assembly in the Sorbonne. Tracking
Michel Corrette: Sonata in D Major, for cello and harpsichord.

*shot of a member of the 'Enragés-SI Committee' and Debord. Board: "Comrades, with
the Sud-Aviation factory in Nantes being occupied for the last two days by the workers
and students of that town, and with the movement being extended today to several
factories (NMPP-Paris, Renault-Cleon, etc), THE SORBONNE OCCUPATION COMMIT-
TEE calls for the immediate occupation of all factories and the formation of workers'
councils. Comrades, broadcast and reproduce this appeal as soon as possible. (Sorbonne, 16 May, 1500 hours)" A mass assembly listen to a speaker in October 1917. The
west front of the Sorbonne garnished with a banner which reads, "Occupy the factories.
For Workers' Councils. (Enragés-SI Committee)" Ports, railway stations and factories
that the strike has paralysed. Board: "And from now on until the end of the world of
the spectacle, the month of May will never return without people remembering us."
Christian Sebastiani. Debord. Patrick Cheval.*

Subtitle in English: We few, we happy few, we band of brothers.

*Graffiti on a fresco by Puvis de Chavannes in the Sorbonne: "Comrades, humanity
will only be happy the day that..." The Sorbonne by night, lights in the windows. The
Winter Palace at night. Leaflets being thrown from the windows of the 'Jules Bonnot
Room', seat of the Sorbonne Occupation Committee. Russian workers, from Eisenstein's October, carrying away packets of leaflets as fast as they come off the
revolutionaries' printing press. Poster on a wall: "Down with the spectacular-com-
modity society." Board: "Don't delude yourself that they haven't such a plan. Of
necessity they have to have it; and if chance dictated that they had not formulated it,
force of circumstance would lead them there; conquest engenders conquest, and victory
thirsts for victory." (Machiavelli, Letter to Francesco Vettori) A few shots of the
occupied Sorbonne; graffiti on a wall: "Run quickly comrade, the old world is behind
you!" Board: "From the 25th February onwards, a thousand strange systems came
issuing pell-mell from the minds of innovators, and spread among the troubled minds
of the mob. It seemed as though the shock of the Revolution had reduced society itself*

Subtitle in English: We few, we happy few,

we band of brothers.

to dust, and as though a competition had been opened for the new form that was to be given to the edifice about to be erected in its place. Everyone came forward with a plan of his own; this one printed it in the newspapers, that one on the posters with which the walls were soon covered, a third proclaimed his loudly at an open air meeting. One aimed at destroying the inequality of wealth, another the inequality of education, a third undertook to do away with the oldest of all inequalities, that between man and woman. Specific remedies were prescribed against poverty and the curse of work which has tortured humanity since the earliest days of its existence." (Alexis de Tocqueville, Memoirs) *A burning barricade at night.*

Subtitle: But neither the wood nor the fire find any peace, satisfaction or ease in any warmth, great or small, or in any kinship, until the moment when the fire becomes one with the wood and they impart to each other their real nature...

Board: "But then what happens is they are accused of vandalism, and their disrespect for the machine is reprimanded and stigmatized. Such criticisms might have some foundation if there was a systematic desire by the workers for destruction without regard for the end. Now that's not the case! If the workers attack machines, it's not for pleasure or out of caprice, but because imperious necessity obliges them to." (Emile Pouget, Sabotage)

Music ends.

The new signs of negation multiplying in the economically most

The CRS in action in the fields around the Flins factory and the streets of Nantes, June

developed countries, signs which are misunderstood and fals-

1968. Young proletarians defending the roofs of St-Jacques.

ified by spectacular arrangement, already enable us to draw the conclusion that a new epoch has begun. After the workers' first attempts at subversion, IT IS CAPITALIST ABUNDANCE WHICH HAS FAILED. When anti-Union struggles of Western workers are repressed first of all by the Unions, and when the first amorphous protests launched by rebellious currents of youth directly imply the rejection of the old specialised politics, of art and of daily life, we see two sides of a spontaneous struggle beginning under a CRIMINAL guise. These are the portents of a second proletarian assault on class society.

A map of Poland. An armoured lorry is set on fire by rioters. A crowd of insurgents climb over the gateway of a palace. In a cafe in Tangiers a woman walks up to a table where a gangster sits and handles his business surrounded by his men. "Do you recognise me?", she asks. He replies, "I never remember pretty women. So, Van Straten has a new yacht". She responds: "It's not a question of business, Tadeusz, but of Poland." He interjects, "I never give in..." but stops in mid-sentence and, as the music from the past gets louder, says emotionally, "Poland".

Board: "Once again Poland is covered in a bloody shroud and we remain powerless spectators." (Declaration of French workers at the founding meeting of the International, 28th September, 1864.)

When constantly growing capitalist alienation at all levels
Street fighting in Italy.

makes it increasingly difficult for workers to recognise and name their own misery, forcing them to face the alternative of rejecting THE TOTALITY OF THEIR MISERY OR NOTHING, the revolutionary organisation has to learn that it can no longer COMBAT ALIENATION WITH ALIENATED MEANS.
Lenin gives a speech.

The very development of class society to the point of spectacular
In Italy police leap from their jeeps and begin truncheoning a crowd of people; West

114

organisation of non-life therefore leads the revolutionary pro-

German security forces operating on foot.

ject to become VISIBLY what it already was ESSENTIALLY.

Revolutionary theory is now the enemy of all revolutionary

Russian tanks push back German workers

ideology, AND KNOWS IT.

in Berlin, June 1953.

A long night sequence: American police truncheon black rioters.

Subtitle: However, let's consider the content of this experience in its entirety; this content is the Work which disappears... The fact of disappearance is also quite real, it becomes attached to the work and itself disappears with it; the negative penetrates the positive of which it is the negation.

Board: "Of course it would be very easy to make history if we only engaged in the struggle with a sure chance of success. To completely destroy this society, it's obviously necessary to be prepared to launch a dozen or more assaults as important as that of May '68, and to consider as unfortunate but inevitable a certain number of defeats and civil wars. The goals which count for something in universal history must be affirmed with energy and willpower."

In the course of a battle in the American Civil War, an officer puts himself at the head of the 7th Michigan cavalry regiment and cries, "Seventh Michigan, advance!... Forward, trot!... Forward, gallop!... Charge!"

Arkadin is holding a masked ball in his Spanish castle. Glass in hand, he says to his guests, "Quiet please. I propose a toast, in the Georgian style. In Georgia, toasts begin with a story... I had a dream of a cemetery where the inscriptions were bizarre: 1822-

1826, 1930-1934... 'People die very young here,' I said to someone, 'there's such a short time between birth and death.' 'No more than elsewhere,' someone replied, 'but here the only years of life that count are those in which friendship has lasted. Let's drink to friendship!" Ivan Chtcheglov. Asger Jorn. The cavalry continue their charge. After the failure of the attack the same officer goes to look for the 5th and 6th Michigan regiments, and throws them into a fresh assault.

Arkadin concludes another story: "'Logical?,' shouted the frog as it swam with the scorpion, 'where is the logic in that?' 'I can't help it,' said the scorpion, 'it's in my character... Let's drink to character!'."

After another setback, the same officer reappears in front of the ranks of the 1st Michigan cavalry, the last reserve, and orders another charge, which begins.

Board: "On the contrary, what constitutes the merit of our theory is not the fact of having had the correct idea, but of having been led quite naturally to conceive of this idea. To sum up, and it should be continually stressed here — as it should in the whole field of practice — theory exists more to train the practitioner and help his judgement, than to serve as an indispensable prop for every step which must be taken for the accomplishment of his task." (Clausewitz, Campaign of 1814)

"Seventh Michigan, advance!"

"I can't help it", said the scorpion, "it's in my character".

Refutation of all judgements
whether for or against,
which have been
brought to date on the film
Society of the Spectacle

1975
SIMAR FILMS

The most tenacious among these discomfited liars, still feigns to wonder whether the society of the spectacle does in fact exist, or whether I am not, by chance, the inventor of it.

The hostility is naturally greater each time that those who are politically reactionary express themselves on my film.

Board inserted into the title sequence: "The critiques most particularly evoked in the present film appeared in 1974 in Le Nouvel Observateur *of 29 April,* Le Quotidien de Paris *of 2 May,* Le Monde *of 9 May,* Télérama *of 11 May,* Le Nouvel Observateur *of 15 May,* Charlie-Hebdo *of 15 May,* Le Point *of 20 May,* Cinéma 74 *of the month of June."*

Epigraph board: "There are times when one should dispense contempt only with the greatest economy, because of the great number of persons in need thereof." Chateaubriand.

The spectacular organisation of modern class society brings

An advertising film touting some beverage or other.

with it two consequences recognisable everywhere: on the one hand, the generalised falsification of products as well as of reasoning; on the other, the obligation, for those who pretend to find their happiness therein, of always maintaining themselves at a great distance from that which they affect to love, for they never possess the means, whether intellectual or otherwise, by which to accede to direct and profound knowledge, a complete praxis and authentic taste.

What is already so apparent when it is a question of living

In a German snack bar, a model train remotely controlled from the cashier's counter

conditions, of wine, of cultural consumption or of the liberation

moves to within arms' reach of the tables, distributing the bill and some mugs of

of morals, should be naturally only the more marked when it is

neo-beer to consumers who joyously drink: for this beverage, if it is chemical in content,

a matter of revolutionary theory, and of the redoubtable lan-

is automated in its delivery.

120

guage which they attach to a condemned world. This naive falsification and this incompetent approbation, which are like the specific odour of the spectacle, have hardly failed to illustrate the commentaries, variously incomprehensible, which have responded to the film entitled *Society of the Spectacle*.

Incomprehension, in this case, imposes itself, for still a bit

Giscard d'Estaing comes out of an old State palace, awaited by numerous photogra-

longer. The spectacle is a poverty, even more than it is a con-

phers and journalists; he gets into his car, which he drives himself.

spiracy. And those who write in the newspapers of our epoch have dissimulated nothing of their intelligence from us. What could they say of pertinence concerning a film which attacks as a whole their habits, their ideas, and which attacks them at the

British troops around a funeral

moment when they themselves begin to feel themselves caving

bier.

in in every detail? The debility of their reactions accompanies the decadence of their world. Those who say that they love this

A couple enters a roadside restaurant, re-

film have loved too many other things to be able to love it; and

spectfully examine the menu, and enjoy an industrial serving of ice cream.

those who say they do not, have themselves accepted too many other things for their judgement to carry the least weight.

One who looks at the poverty of their life understands quite well the poverty of their discourse. It is enough to see their set

Advertising film; various automobiles

decorations and their occupations, their commodities and their

crash on a highway, which they almost completely block; but the one with the good

ceremonies; and that is spread out everywhere. It's enough to

tyres, arriving at a formidable speed, zig zags its way through the obstruction without

hear these imbecilic voices which tell you that you have become

slowing down and moves off elegantly.

alienated, as they inform you of it with contempt, at every hour
that passes.

Advertising film: a strip-tease with several young women, to hype one knows not what kind of commodity. This ad is enriched by the voice of a radio announcer who placidly describes, as if it were the most normal thing in the world, the delays, bottlenecks, the times of the delays, at this moment known to the listeners on the highways to which they have delivered themselves en masse on holiday.

Spectactors do not find what they desire: they desire what they

Advertising film: A customer enters a luxurious English store.

find.

He is welcomed with respectful eagerness. He is shown cigarettes of different lengths and is given one to try. He finds it too long. It is cut. It is still a bit too long. It is shortened again. He is presented with a mirror. The customer contemplates himself in it with the cigarette in his mouth. He declares himself satisfied.

The spectacle does not debase men to the point of making them

Now an ordinary package of cigarettes is placed in his hand, of the very same length.

love it; but many are paid to pretend they do. Now that they

April 1974 in Por-

122

can no longer go so far as to ensure that this society is fully

tugal: soldiers, carnations in their rifles, marching, passing by on lorries; sailors mixed

satisfactory, they hurry first to declare themselves dissatisfied

in amongst civilian demonstrators.

with all critique of that which exists. All dissatisfied individuals

At the podium of the Cannes Film

believe that they deserve better. But did they imagine, then, that

Festival, the best actors, directors etc, receive their recompense.

someone was trying to convince them? Do they believe that there would still be time for them to ally themselves with such a critique, if, all of a sudden, it carried off their adherence? Do they believe themselves able to speak, while causing it to be forgotten from whence they speak, themselves the ill-lodged inhabitants of the territory of approbation?

That would be a subject for astonishment, in a future more free and more truthful, that those employed in the writing of the system of spectacular lies should be capable of believing themselves qualified to render their opinion, and tranquilly weigh the pros and cons, concerning a film which is a negation of the spectacle; as if the dissolution of this system was an affair of opinions. Their system is now attacked in reality; it defends itself by force; the counterfeit coin of their arguments has no currency, and so unemployment currently threatens a good

The film director Costa Gavras, on this fine day.

number of the cadres of falsification.

The most tenacious among these discomfited liars, still feigns

Panorama over a great accumulation of television screens, upon which are simulta-

to wonder whether the society of the spectacle does in fact exist,

neously projected all the sporting events of the Olympic Games in Munich.

or whether I am not, by chance, the inventor of it. However,

Demonstration

Subtitle: Lisbon,

since for several years the forest of history has begun to march

of Portuguese workers; blockades o tanks and soldiers are deployed to contain them.

7 February 1975. Thirty-eight federated factories condemn the stalinists, the

against their castle of false cards, and continues at this very

unions, and the ministers.

moment to close up its ranks against the investment, nearly all
these commentators currently possess the baseness to hail the
excellence of my book, as if they were capable of reading it, and
as if they had welcomed it with such respect in 1967. However,

A series of

they generally find that I abuse their indulgence in bringing this

television screens juxtaposed; long sequence of closer-in shots of one competition or

book to the screen. And the blow is the more painful to them in

another. Only human weakness prevents one seeing everything at once; or at least

that they had in no way imagined that such an excess was

seeing everything related to those particular games.

possible. Their anger confirms that the appearance of such a
critique in the cinema disturbs them even more than in a book.

There, as elsewhere, they find themselves constrained to fight in retreat, along a second line of defence. Many blame this film for being difficult to understand. According to several, the images prevent the words from being heard, if it's not the other way around. In saying that this film exhausts them, and in proudly arrogating to their personal exhaustion the general criterion of communication, they would like first to give the impression that they understand without difficulty, that they nearly approve the same theory when given exposition in a book. And so they attempt to disguise as a simple disagreement over a conception of the cinema, that which is, in truth, a conflict over a conception of society; and an open war in society as it actually exists.

But why then should they understand, and any better than a film which surpasses them, all the rest which escapes them in a society which has perfectly conditioned them to mental exhaustion? How then should their weakness find itself in any better posture to discern amidst the uninterrupted noise of so many simultaneous messages of advertising and of the government, all of the crude sophisms which tend to make them accept their work and their leisure pursuits, the thought of President Giscard and the taste of amyloids? The difficulty is not in my film but in their prostrated heads.

No film is more difficult than its epoch. For example, there are people who understand, and others who do not understand, that when the French were offered, according to a very old recipe of power, a new minister called 'Minister of the Quality of Life', that it was simply, as Machiavelli said, "in order that they should retain at least the name of that which they had lost". There are those people who understand, and others who do not

During the first days of the Portuguese revolution, the stalinist Cunhal, the socialist

understand, that the class struggle in Portugal was from the

Soares, General Spinola, and whoever else held onto any shred of authority, come

beginning and principally dominated by the direct contention

forward one after the other to register publicly, in the reflected lustre of a national

between the revolutionary workers organised into autonomous

palace, their commitment to do all they can to prevent this revolution from proceeding

assemblies, and the stalinist bureaucracy enriched by generals

further.

in flight from defeat. Those who understand this are the same ones who are able to understand my film; and I am not making a film for those who do not understand, or who feign not to understand that.

Though all the commentaries come from the same zone pol-

Series of oil wells with flares.

luted by the industry of the spectacular, they are, like the

Brief sequence on a mod-

commodities of today, apparently varied. Several have af-

ern cattle farm: the chemistry and the associated automation for bringing the milk and

firmed that they have been filled with enthusiasm by this film,

the meat of this livestock to a degree of quality worthy of the contemporary consumer.

and they have sought in vain to say why. Each time I find myself

Long tracking shot around an

approved by those people who should be my enemies, I ask

oil exploration platform, which deep-sea tugs are putting into position.

myself what error they have themselves committed in their reasonings. It is generally easy to find. Encountering a strange quantity of novelties, and an insolence which they cannot even understand, some consumers of the *avant-garde* seek here to approach an impossible approbation by reconstructing some pretty bizarreries with an individual lyricism which was not there.

Thus, one tries to admire in my film "a lyricism of rage"; another

Various nebulae.

has discovered there that the passage of an historical epoch brought with it a certain melancholy; others, who assuredly overestimate the refinements of current social life, attribute to me a certain dandyism. In all of this, that old scoundrel of yesteryear pursues "his mania FOR DENYING WHAT IS, AND FOR EXPLAINING WHAT IS NOT". The critical theory which accompanies the dissolution of a society does not give itself up to rage, and it should have even less to do with showing the simple image of it. It understands, describes, and employs itself to

Portuguese workers' demonstration: "Down with the provisional government."

precipitate a movement which actually unreels in front of our very eyes. As for those who present us with their pseudo-rage as a sort of artistic material come into the world, one knows that they seek by those means only to compensate for the pliability, the compromise and the humiliations of their life as it really is; with which spectators will find little difficulty in identifying themselves.

The hostility is naturally greater each time that those who are

The stalinist Cunhal, on a tribune with several of his accomplices, resolutely intones

politically reactionary express themselves on my film. It is thus

some lying political slogan.

that an apprentice bureaucrat seeks to offer approbation of my

Soares, in the role of the mild democrat, smiles at everyone; receives flowers, holds

audacity in "making a political film, not by telling a story, but

boring meetings.

by filming theory directly". However, he does not like my theory at all. He sniffs out that, in the guise of "the left without concessions". I will instead slide to the right, and it's because I systematically attack "the men of the united left". These are precisely the exaggerated words with which the mouth of this cretin is full. What union? What left? What men?

It is merely, and quite notoriously, the union of the stalinists with other enemies of the proletariat. Each of the partners knows well the other, they plot awkwardly among themselves, and raise a great hue and cry accusing each other every week; but they hope to be able still to plot together against all the revolutionary initiatives of the workers, in order to maintain, as

128

it is convenient for them, the essentials of capitalism, even if they don't manage to rescue all the details. It is they who repress in Portugal, as but a short while ago in Budapest, the 'counter-revolutionary strikes' of the workers; the same ones who aspire to make themselves 'compromise historically' in Italy; the same ones who called themselves the Popular Front when they broke the strikes of 1936 and the Spanish revolution.

A crowd at a meeting, waving red flags. Filmed by les Actualités 12 July 1936, Salengro speaks at the tribune of a socialist meeting. A small, ridiculous

Subtitle: The so-

and odious man, doing all that he can to give himself a Mussolini-style, he declares:
cialist Roger Salengro, Minister of the Interior of the Popular Front.

"Order, we will uphold; in leading the working class to understand that its duty and its interest command it to hear our appeals, and to prevent us from having recourse to means of constraint. No, the Popular Front will not be anarchy! The Popular Front will live, the Popular Front will triumph only insofar as it is able to ensure order. It is necessary for the working class to be capable of understanding that its duty and its interests require that it do nothing which will set against it the middle class and the peasant class. The day after tomorrow, in a great procession, the three colours of the nation and the red flag of labour will be united. This 14 July, the day of the Republic, the day of the proletariat, we will ask the people of Paris to watch over its victory of April and May. We will ask the people of France to maintain its confidence in the

Subtitle: Four months later, an extreme right would push to

government: in a government which only lives through the people, in a government
suicide, through several slanders, this man who had only the strength to
which only lives for the people and which will only triumph to the extent that the
scorn his electors.

People of France help it to do so".

The united left is but the trivial defensive mystification of

The stalinist Cunhal, looking ill at ease.

spectacular society, because the system makes use of it only occasionally. I evoked it only in passing in my film; but, of course, I attack it with the contempt that it merits; as we have

A cordon of Portuguese soldiers, at the top of a monumental stairway,

since attacked it in Portugal, on a more attractive and more vast

protecting the palace of the government, at nightfall.

terrain. A journalist near to that same left, who since achieved

News agency telex; technical equipment of a radio station; its studio etc.

a certain notoriety in justifying himself for having published an improbable false document because it is thus that he conceives the freedom of the press, is engaged in equally abject forgery when he insinuates that I would not have attacked the bureaucrats of Peking as clearly as the other ruling classes. He deplores besides, that a mind of my quality should content itself with a "ghetto cinema", that the masses will have little occasion to see.

In Lisbon, a demonstration by textile workers.

The argument will not convince me: I prefer to remain in the shadow, with the masses, rather than to agree to harangue them with the artificial lighting that their hypnotists manipulate.

Another equally modestly gifted jesuit pretends, on the contrary, to wonder whether if to denounce the spectacle would not itself be to enter into the spectacle? One may easily see what such an extraordinary purism would like to obtain: that no one should ever appear in the spectacle as an enemy.

Those who have not even a subaltern post to lose in spectacular

In a university restaurant, the filling up of trays.

society, but only their ambitious hope to act as the most juvenile

Advertising film: in a de-

relief thereto, have displayed more frankly and more furiously

sert landscape, young men and women dressed in hippie garb gaily follow a bearded

their discontent, and even their jealousy. An extremely repre-

young man who walks a little ahead. Encountering an expanse of water, the bearded

sentative anonymous individual has for quite some time pro-

one walking first goes forth nonchalantly and walks on the waters, thanks to his 'Buggy

mulgated the theses of the most recent conformism, in their

d'Eram' shoes. Others follow him, equally well-shod, so that the miracle is repeated.

natural place, that is to say in the weekly of the humourists of

But those of little faith who didn't believe in 'Buggy d'Eram' sink into the water up

the old guard of the Mitterandist electorate.

to their knees and remain behind with no-one turning back for them.

This anonymous individual finds that it would have been very

Giscard d'Estaing welcomes the Portuguese Head of State: Chirac follows: a squad of

well to film my book in 1967, but that in 1973 it was too late. He

troops does the honours.

offers in proof the fact that it seems urgent to him to leave off
talking about everything of which he is ignorant: Marx; Hegel;
books in general, because they cannot be an adequate instrument of emancipation; any employment of the cinema; theory

even more than the rest; and history itself, from which he rejoices to have anonymously departed.

A thought so decomposed could obviously only have oozed

In a university restaurant, students line up for the distribution of neo-nourishment.

forth from the desolate walls of Vincennes. Within living memory, one has never seen a theory born from a student at Vincennes. And it is precisely there that one finds advocated, at least provisionally so it seems, anti-theory. What else should they sell

Amphitheatres full of certified neo-

in exchange for an assistant professorship in the neo-university

thinkers.

sity? Not that they content themselves with that, the least well-

Cyclists arrive, racing at top speed.

endowed of the recuperator degree candidates today going everywhere ringing doorbells thinking to become at least the editor of a collection at a publishing house, and if possible a film

The victor,

director: that anonymous individual, moreover, does not hide

with a garland of flowers.

his envy of what in his eyes are the ostentatious profits of the cinema. One may rest assured that not one of these anti-theories

Tracking shot over the harbour of an industrial zone.

will easily attain the silence, which is its only authentic accomplishment, because then its purveyors would be no more than employees without qualifications. This anonymous individual

Advertising film, touting a brand of trou-

in fact lays his cards on the table at the end. The imposter had

sers: on the stage of a music hall, some men dress themselves up in new clothes to the

wished to dissolve history only in order to choose another. And

accompaniment of music, to the applause of a feminine audience.

this death's head advances with the names of Lyotard, Castoriadis, and other crumb gatherers in tow; that is to say, people
who had given their best fifteen years ago, without managing
to particularly dazzle their century.

*Advertising film touting iced tea. Confederate cavalry are leaving for the war. They
leave their houses and their parties behind. One who has never known this has never
known the good things in life, etc. A conclusion of Hegelian brutality: "Their
civilisation has disappeared. All that remains of them is iced tea."*

No loser ever loves history. And on the other hand, when one

Confederate officers, at a garden party in the same advertising film; dignified old

denies history at home, why should the most resolutely inno-

gentlemen, a faithful black servant brings the iced tea; couples making vain plans.

vative careerism be troubled by sidling up to recuperated men
in their fifties? Why should one see that it is contradictory to
give oneself out as anonymous who has remained so utterly
silent after 1968 and to admit that one has not even arrived at
despising the professoriat? This anonymous individual has all

In Portugal soldiers break up a demonstration.

the same the merit of having illustrated better that the others
the ineptitude of the anti-historical reflection with which he
advertises himself; as the real intentions of this false contempt

that the powerless oppose to reality. In postulating that it was too late to undertake a cinematic adaptation of *Society of the Spectacle* six years after the appearances of this book, he neglects first of all the fact that there have doubtless not been three books

Yankee marauders enter a luxurious Southern mansion, pillage

of social critique of such importance in the last hundred years.

it and set it on fire.

He forgets besides that I had myself written the book. All terms of comparison are lacking to evaluate whether I was slow or fast, since it is patently obvious that the best of my detractors do not make use of the cinema. So, I must admit, I found it quite good to be the first to realise this sort of exploit.

The defenders of the spectacle will come to recognise in it this

In Portugal a loudspeaker installed on a tank exhorts the crowd to calm.

new employment of the cinema as slowly as they came to recognise the fact that a new epoch of revolutionary struggle

Protestors intone their demands; in the front line a

saps their society; but they will be constrained to recognise it

little girl more convinced than anyone. At the funeral of the most recent king of

just as inevitably. Following the same course, at first they re-

England, troops pass by in parade, holding their rifles upside down. Highlanders,

main silent; then they speak around their subject. The commen-

marines, grenadiers, Horse Guards, in the ancient costumes which saw the power and

tators of my film have reached this stage.

the glory of the Empire, accompany a coffin surmounted by the orb and sceptre.

The specialists of the cinema said that its revolutionary politics were bad; the politicians among all the left-wing illusionists said that it was bad cinema. But when one is at once a revolutionary and a film-maker, one may easily demonstrate that their general bitterness derives from the obvious fact that the film in question is the exact critique of the society which they do not know how to combat; and a first example of the cinema which they do not know how to make.

"Order, we will uphold; in leading the working class to understand that its duty and its interest command it to hear our appeals, and to prevent us from having recourse to means of constraint. No, the Popular Front will not be anarchy!"

The imposter had wished to dissolve history only in order to choose another. And this death's head advances with the names of Lyotard, Castoriadis, and other crumb gatherers in tow...

No loser ever loves history.

136

The specialists of the cinema said that its revolutionary politics were bad; the politicians among all the left-wing illusionists said that it was bad cinema.